The Book of GLAM

Tara L. Paige

Acknowledgement

I would like to take a moment to thank MY God for planting this seed so deep within me. I am most gracious that I was chosen to go through the darkest days with you by my side. I know there were times when I thought my life was worthless, but you continued to trust me with dreams only I could birth. I am blessed by you and I give you all the glory. My God, this is for you!

Secondly, this dream would not be perfect without my great team: I love you all!

Dedication

To My husband, Reginald, who is my earthly peace! I thank you from the depths of my soul for all you have done and will do! I am thankful for your spirit and your willingness to always take care of me. I love you more than more than! You are my everything!

To my mom and dad! I do not have enough tongues to reach an infinite ocean of thank you's! I am so grateful for your rights and wrongs! Through it all you have created a resilient daughter. It is what you have instilled in me that has carried me through the deepest point of my life, and allowed me to rise to the pinnacle of success! I am blessed!

Grandma, I am so humbly blessed to have just celebrated 100 years with you. I am very eager to celebrate 101. I adore our long talks, love our infectious laughter and cherish our visits. It is you that I strive to mimic, for you are the epitome of a Queen. I love you, Grandma!

To my children who have been hanging onto my wings, no matter the ride. I thank you for hanging on! You are my greatest gifts! I am blessed!

Preface

I never thought it would be possible to pull myself up from the darkest place. I was somewhere unbeknownst to man, unbeknownst to life. I was without air and I found it very hard to breathe. I didn't believe I was capable of living a better life than the one I was dished and yet the strange thing is, I never felt *comfortable* in the life I was in. I felt like I was destined for greater, but couldn't access it as I was stuck in a rut. My self-esteem was low, my self-worth was zero and I thought that maybe that was where I was supposed to be - unhappy, sad, depressed, angry, and unhealthy and always peeking in the window of others' happiness.

Now that was the last straw. I listened to a voice within me say, "you're supposed to be happy too!" I looked around, trying to figure out where this voice was coming from. Who knows, it could have been the whistle of the wind, but I took it to be the sweet voice of my Heavenly Father reminding me that I could have anything I wanted, if I just asked for it, so I decided to do *just that*. I went boldly with demands that *only* my Heavenly Father could fulfil.

Sure, I was out of my league - I was uncomfortable and I was afraid. I was definitely emotional, but I wasn't sad or depressed, and that *meant the world* to me. I was preparing myself to prosper beyond my normal means. I was about to be shown how faith can take you places both high and low. I was no longer afraid of taking the leap, in fact I jumped confidently into this new life, knowing that my parachute would release when needed, and I would have a good landing.

Being confident didn't mean that I wasn't afraid - it meant that my fear was my fuel. I used my fear to propel me to new heights. When it's time to make something happen, you can use your fear to stop yourself, or use that fear to fuel your journey. I took the latter. I've jumped and now I'm ready to conquer the world. This method is not here just to work for me - **this can work for you too.** You must see yourself on the path you want to travel and **kick fear into gear**, allowing it to propel you forward.

Let's get one thing straight – even successful people FAIL. So prepare yourself to launch, prepare yourself to fail and have fear, but ALSO prepare yourself to be successful, knowing that you're destined for far greater things to come. HAVE FAITH!

Table of Contents

The Book of Being Lost

Y ou will quickly come to realize that I am a very spiritual person with strong beliefs in what is right and wrong. I cannot underestimate the power of prayer and what it has done for me; it has literally transformed my life! The knowledge that I will always have a listening ear to whisper into and a shoulder to cry on is astonishing, especially in a world where, (all too often,) no-one else cares. I thought I would share with you some of my favorite prayers and hope they bring as much comfort and inspiration to you as they have done to me. You will find them at the end of each book.

I'm not gonna lie; being a single mother isn't easy. But you don't need *me* to tell you that. When life throws you an unexpected pregnancy, you may feel like you want to hide in shame or pretend like it's not happening. Where you are is not a secret place. It's not uncharted territory. You're not the first woman to be in this position, and sure as eggs are eggs, you're not gonna be the last! Many women lose their way at this time, and find themselves in a situation they can't wrap their heads around. It's scary, it's new and it's daunting. What you need to remember is that no matter how lost you feel, you *can* find your way. I remember as a single mother, I had no clue about what I had really gotten myself into. I didn't understand the magnitude of being a mother and having a little person depend on me for *everything*.

I know your pain. I know your fear. I know your struggles. I've been there. I've cried, I've screamed, and been in a dark place where I felt lost, alone and without direction. What you're dealing with is real, and I'm sure you probably feel like no one understands. You have all of these questions and fears swimming around inside your head, but no answers to anything. It's only natural to feel overwhelmed, and it is easy to allow that "lost" feeling to bury you if you allow it to.

Many of us have felt like you do at this moment; feeling like there's no support - from family, friends, or from the father of your child. That moment you found out for certain that you were with child, what did you feel? Was it fear? An all-encompassing feeling of sickness and dread? I'll bet it was a feeling of "lost" on a whole other level. Trust me; I know that the fear starts before you even set that stick down that reads, "Pregnant".

Why do you feel this way? Because now it's real and you have to tell people. You have to tell the father, first off, and that in itself is a very scary feeling. Especially if you all are not already in a committed relationship. You may be afraid that he is going to abandon you, leaving you and the baby alone... All sorts of frightening scenarios run through your mind, such as hearing him say, "I don't wanna be with you", *after* you tell him that you're carrying his precious child.

The knowledge that you will have to take care of his baby while he is out partying, dating, and basically going on with his life without you or your child will weigh heavy in your heart and soul. Especially when you had those princess dreams of getting married to him and having a "happily ever after" with your family.

Or worse still; what about if he asks you to get an abortion? Just the idea of it can seem unthinkable and you won't want to give any room inside your head to allow that thought to linger. But it happens. It happened to *me* twice, and each time it took me to a dark place. If you do experience the unfortunate instance of the father suggesting an abortion to you, you're definitely gonna feel hurt and scared. Just hearing him utter those words will take you to an uncomfortable place, to an unfamiliar place with this man that you had been intimate with. It makes you feel lonely and alone.

I was eighteen the first time I heard those dreaded words, and I remember a cold feeling spreading right through me.

There was no emotion on his part and no concern at all for me, or for his baby. He didn't think of me; I can see now that he was only thinking of himself and his future. I was young, scared, and confused. All I wanted was for him to make me feel like we were going through this together, and that I could lean on him. Make me feel like I was worth something after letting him into the most intimate places in my mind, body and soul. And I didn't get that, all I got was fear and the knowledge that I was on my own, and that's a lonely thing to feel.

Whether someone is there for you or not, you *have* to roll with the punches; you have no choice in the matter. Sure, you're gonna cry, you're gonna hurt, you're gonna feel bad. But you're the hero now. There is a child, this little person, looking at you like you're wearing a red cape and have an 'S' on your chest. And you know what? You need to embrace it, because that's *who you are now.* Okay, so your pregnancy was unplanned, but it was *not* unloved and not unwanted, once conception had taken place. Becoming a parent, (especially a single one,) means that you have to accept your choices, and live with the results of them as your life evolves day by day and month by month.

As women, we feel so connected to men when we lay down with them. Men don't necessarily feel that connection all the time, but we, as nurturers, develop a deeper connection which goes way beyond the physical. We welcome men into our most sacred place, only to be devastated when they leave us behind as if we were nothing. We become hurt and angry. That pain makes us become bitter and to say, "I don't trust anybody." But you have to ask yourself, "How do I create a way to move forward? How do I move away from this lost feeling? Will it ever end?"

All these emotions are raging through you at the most delicate time - when you're a miraculous incubator for the most precious gift known to man. You've just been blessed with the opportunity to be a mommy. Not *everyone* gets that opportunity. I know that it's easier said than done, but negative emotions raging inside of you at this time will *not* help your baby. If you feel stressed, then so do they. Don't allow this man's negativity to affect your precious cargo; your baby deserves so much more than that.

This is an opportunity for you to move forward. This is the time to re-evaluate who you are, and what *he* really is about. This is the time to really understand who you are, and who you want, (and will allow, from now on,) into your innermost circle. It's done now. So how do you move forward? How do you make the best of it? How do you continue without this pain and learn to move beyond it?

Well, let's be honest here; you *won't* get rid of the pain overnight, life unfortunately doesn't work that way. But you have to remember, (and keep telling yourself,) that he is worthless and no good for you and he does not deserve for you to spend too much time dwelling on him and what might have been. **Real men** stand up, no matter what. Whatever the situation may be, they're gonna stand up. Take note, though: they may not stand up *right now*, but they will in time. So this *isn't* the time to create hate for them - this is the time to forgive and love. You have a precious child to raise - you have an important job to do. You don't have time to focus on him. Your job is to focus on yourself, seek God, and then let Him focus on crafting the perfect mate for you.

And then comes the horrifying realization that you have to tell your parents that not only are you pregnant, but are also unwed. I don't know about you, but I grew up with parents that always told me to keep my legs closed; that was it – no further advice or assistance about how to cope with sexual feelings which can sweep through you even though you know it's wrong to allow them to happen. There was no help about what to do when your man tells you, "If you loved me you would..." I *knew* they would be disappointed, and it took me about two to three weeks to get up the nerve to tell them.

My life plans had always included getting married and having children, and I looked forward to the day when I would be proud to say, "Mom, I'm pregnant!" I envisioned a solid marriage, possibly a white picket fence, a two-car garage and a barking dog; the whole nine yards in fact! However, as I grew older and more mature, I recognized that lifelong plans are not *always* the reality that we end up living. If only it were that simple; we would all be able to wave that magic wand and our lives would be perfect! If only! In fact, there is a saying that goes, "If you want to make God laugh, tell Him what your plans are"!

I know that telling your parents is going to be a scary moment for you, but believe me, you're strong enough to get through it...YOU ARE! At the end of the day, you're going to feel like a target. You may feel like all eyes are on you and that you're being judged everywhere you go. You know what? It's *natural* to feel emotional, and like you're unable to confront this situation. This is real, and it will hit you like a ton of bricks. Right now, it's about you and your willingness to make it, though.

Your parents will have their own feelings, ideas and decisions about what they would do in a particular situation, and they are unlikely to be the same as yours. But that's okay – we're all different and our life experiences can make us react in different ways to a situation. That's why your parents' reaction may be what it is. And while that may be a factor, you can't hang your hat on their decisions or reactions, especially when they are not directly involved in the situation. Sure, you can be respectful and listen to them but at the end of the day, this is your life and you have to do what is right for *you* and your baby.

There is no 'perfect' reaction to any situation; we're *all* different and we've all made mistakes. Your only 'mistake' (if it can be called that!) was an action that will soon produce a gift that will call you "mommy". Most people's reactions are going to be in response to the fear they have themselves. The louder they fuss, the more they cuss... they're really scared. While it might not *seem* like they're fearful because they're lashing out at you – the truth is, it's simply fear; fear for you; fear for the future; fear of what their friends and peers are going to think and how they will react to the news. There will be shame, there will be embarrassment, but none of these are emotions which will last or have a harming effect on you in the long term. So go in, deal with it, and time heals all wounds... I promise.

There are no promises in relationships, not even friendships. You might be afraid to tell your friends because you're scared that they will think of you as worthless. Maybe they'll talk about you behind your back and say things about you messing up your life. Sometimes we're afraid that we're not able to be a part of the crew any more, and want to reconsider our decisions. You might find yourself feeling hopeless, scared and anxious, but ask yourself this: what is the definition of a true friend?

> *"When life deals you a rough hand, it's not about how strong you are, but how many people out there believe in you, stand by you: your FRIENDS."* – Aman Jassal, 'Rainbow - the shades of love.'

A true friend does not judge you - they stand by you. A true friend will not demean you, backstab you, or be two-faced. Instead, they will lift you up, and be determined to help you get through this process. These so-called "friends" of yours who will walk away?... SO WHAT! It's time to re-evaluate you.

It's ok that they walked away; they needed to. Don't worry about it; those that matter will still be by your side and in it for the long-haul. You don't need to babysit a friendship. Relationships are here to enhance your life, not break it down or make you feel bad. Find peace in knowing that God will be getting rid of the trash in your life. After all, it keeps you from having to deal with it later on down the road. And remember, the more trash sticks around, the stinkier it becomes. NO ONE WANTS OR NEEDS STINKY TRASH!!! And when it's gone, it's gone for good. Chin up, sugar. This is an opportunity to begin something new. This is your time to shine, so shine bright like a diamond! Onwards and upwards! Who needs negativity? Certainly not you; you have new paths to follow!

Society is really good at making us feel bad about lots of things we do; pregnancy outside of marriage being a major issue for many people. We would do well to remember the saying, "let he who is without sin cast the first stone". No-one is perfect and yet all too many people take the moral high ground and somehow manage to assume that makes them better than you or I. Instead of taking a look at the absent father and his role in all of this, it's too easy to cast negative images on the mother. We tend to view her as someone who has been irresponsible, loose, and, somehow, isn't too smart.

This makes it so easy for single mothers to fall into a downward spiral of shame. There's so much on your plate to deal with. You're *already* dealing with the feeling that you've disappointed your family, your friends don't want to hang around you anymore, and you're getting those "looks" of judgment out in public, which are really getting under your skin.

Whatever the case may be, you have to stand tall and keep your head held high. What other choice do you have? You're not here to be an object of ridicule or shame; you're here for a reason. A purpose that you just might not have realized yet, but God has! Look at your swollen belly with pride.

Don't accept the blanket of shame that the outside world is trying to put on you. Refuse it! Accept your mistakes and find forgiveness within yourself. You are a queen, and God ordained you to birth that wonderful child you have. God chose you to guide that child's development. That is an honor; not something to be ashamed of!

This place you are in at the moment - it can be so hard, I know. It can feel like you're drowning in the abyss of the deepest ocean, and you can't surface for air. Your arms don't work, your legs don't work and no matter how hard you try and pull yourself up, nothing works. You wonder where you can go next and whether it's even worth the effort of trying to get there anymore. You may have those deep, dark moments where you feel like death would be an easier choice. Like leaving it all behind and not having to give it a second thought would be the better answer; the easier option. I'm telling you, it's not! You may be hurting, but you're still here.

And always remember that you're here for a reason - because **no-one else** could bring this child into the world but you. Sure, life may have thrown you a curve ball, but don't you know that God is in the Major Leagues and he is a master batting coach? *He* has coached you on how to swing for the fence. He has coached you on the GRAND SLAM technique. So now the bases are loaded, and it's *up* to you to bring everyone in. This is *your* scenario. This is *your* life and *you* are up to bat. This is *your* chance to show God that his gift is wanted and you will do *everything* in your power to take care of it.

> *"Your children are the greatest gift God will give to you and their souls the heaviest responsibility He will place in your hands. Take time with them; teach them to have faith in God. Be a person in whom they can have faith. When you are old, **nothing else** you've done will have mattered as much."* – Lisa Wingate.

You can't worry about people and what they think or say behind your back. You just can't and do you know why? Because you are now at a point in your life where you have no choice but to find yourself. Continuing to linger and dwell in this space of being lost with no hope is **no longer an option**. Now is the time to lean on God and allow him to show you, through discernment, who is right for you and who's not. Sit back for a while and let this feeling sweep through you; embrace this moment wholeheartedly - this is an opportunity to start anew. This is your chance to hit that home run for God. Remember, you have been taught by the best.

I can say these things with confidence because I *know* what it's like when you've reached that lowest point. I *know* how dragged down you can be by life in general. And although it was darned hard, when I reached my rock bottom I knew I was the only one who could climb back up from it. My rock bottom looked something like this: The man I wanted dearly, I could not have. I was about 150 pounds overweight. Yes, I had been blessed with healthy children, but I was still doing it on my own. I was living the "struggle of the juggle", because, (as we all know,) mothers can easily perform 40 to 50 different tasks a day. Plus, my finances were spiralling out of control because of how much I was trying to manage with haphazard organization and pack-rat tendencies. Oh yeah, something had to give, and I was determined that it would not be me crumbling under the pressure.

And that was easier said than done. When you're juggling and trying to keep all the balls in the air, you become very good at lying to yourself and your kids. You keep telling yourself that you're okay; you can manage. You tell your kids that you're not hungry because you ate earlier; you'll have something when they are in bed. You smile and say "No, that's all thanks," when you go to the grocery store and the assistant asks you if you want anything else. In reality, you are mentally counting the pennies in your wallet, hoping that you have enough to pay for what you have. You go home and tuck the kids into bed, making sure that they are warm enough and then sit there with your coat on because you have no money for electricity. I know; I've been there.

When you're a single parent, you carry everything on your shoulders all alone, and the stress wears on you. It affects how you eat, your sleeping habits, how you see yourself, and how you see life. Those behaviors become a reflection of how much care and value you place on yourself, and after a while, it shows. It's not about just transforming your look - it's more than just the glam on the outside... what about the glam on the inside? Remember, you have to love you for you. Your goal is to get back to a place of happiness and love that lifts you away from rock bottom, and it starts with the **choices you make for yourself.**

"Dear God, I am lost and I need your help right now. I am somewhere I don't want to be and I am asking your help to bring me out. I know you love me and want the best for me. I now know this and want the best you have for me. Dear God I no longer want to be lost. Help me find myself and you within me, In Jesus name Amen."

The Book of Acceptance

"You are who you are. Period. And you are beautiful." It feels good when somebody says that to you, but when you're all alone and saying it to yourself, it can be hard to believe sometimes. It helps if you have someone to keep reinforcing that message but when you're on your own, that's not easy to come by. Insecurities we hold about ourselves make us hide behind an image which makes it easier for us to face the world. How often have you carefully applied your make-up to create a 'mask' which you can hide behind? How often have you purposefully plastered a smile on your face when all you really feel like doing is crying? If we feel like we don't fit society's standards, we do all this changing to suit the audience, but *don't* manage to address the root problems that made us feel so insecure in the first place. And if we *don't* manage to do that, then we will keep on going round and round in circles and *never* feeling any better.

Healing and accepting starts with being honest with yourself, and *not* hiding behind those little lies we all tell ourselves from time to time. There comes a time when you have to face the truth and accept that a change needs to take place. You will realize that you have to stop running from your problems and **face them head-on**. Accept your flaws, confident in the knowledge that no-one is perfect, but also accept your beauty and worth. Self-acceptance involves two main things: cleaning your core and ridding yourself of poisonous people and things.

I am a strong believer in karma or the Laws of Attraction; call it what you will. But basically this means that what you put out into this world, that's *exactly* what you will get back. Think of it as 'an eye for an eye and a tooth for a tooth'. If you surround yourself with negative people, then they will eventually drag you down and you will feel unable to escape from that constant merry-go-round of feeling that nothing is worth doing, because it never works out anyway. Whereas, if you surround yourself with positive people who reinforce the message that 'anything is possible' you will come to realize that is true – anything IS possible, especially if you work hard at it! You have to learn to accept what your new life is going to be and *embrace the change*. I understand that it *will* be challenging, but you're left with no choice; this is the way things *have* to be from now on.

When I say cleaning your core, I mean giving yourself to God and understanding that He is the root of your joy. Your core is the innermost part of you; the part that only God gets to see in its entirety. Change *has* to start from within that deep place. But in order for that change to occur, you have to let God into your core, allowing him in without fear or preconceived ideas as to what he will think of this secret place.

Cleaning it all out is simply letting go of all things weighing you down, and turning to him for everything. It's about *not* being afraid to go to him with your requests, and being patient while you wait for your answer. You've already been at that point where you *tried* to do it yourself and *not* lean on God for all things. How did that work? My guess is that your answer to that would be, "not so good!"

Well, now it's time to lean on someone who can truly help. It's time to give it all to God... all the pain, all the stress, all the burdens, all the anger. Hand it over to him and his arms will *willingly* accept every last bit. When you let go and let God in, life becomes more peaceful. Don't allow *anything or anyone* to taint your path from this point on. It's all been wiped clean. This is a new beginning, and now you can truly accept YOU and learn to fall in love with the perfect being you are.

In order to make repairs, don't you have to know where the problems are? Don't you need to know what's broken? If you call a plumber out to your house for service, you don't want him to just start messing around with pipes and shutting off your water without knowing what the problem is, right? In order for him to do his job and make repairs, he's got to know what's broken. Well the same is true for what is going on inside of you; to move forward, you need to know what wants fixing.

The transition from being lost to arriving at a place of acceptance *isn't easy*, and the reality is that God plays a major role in that transition. That glimmer of light that brings you out of the darkness? That's God's presence, and he's letting you know that he'll *always* be there. That alone gives you the strength to make it through another day. You may not think too highly of yourself right now, but know that you are a child of God, and that acceptance that you're not perfect and the ability to love yourself *will* come in time.

Consider this: what if joy comes from within, where God lives—where He created us? That joy has absolutely *nothing* to do with the choices you've made or the circumstances you may have found yourself in. That joy has *everything* to do with God being perfect, and the joy He's placed within all of us is perfect. It has nothing to do with what you look like on the outside - it starts on the inside. God pays no heed to outward appearances; he knows that it's what's on the inside that counts. Realize that God *can* give joy, even in the darkest moments. I found joy in God, who lives in me, and so can you. You can talk to Him and find peace in any situation. When I asked for guidance, He calmed me.

So one of the most important steps you can take today is to stop focusing so much on what you look like on the outside; it's not important. Start focusing on who is on the inside. Are you a nice person? Do you try your best to treat others as you want to be treated? Do you try to always be truthful and honest? Do you know how to love, and to love with all of your heart? When you focus on the inside then you'll find rest *and* peace within yourself. God will whisper for you to be still, and sometimes He will silence you to sleep. When that happens, heed His instructions. I know those quiet, serene times really helped me, especially when I was dealing with the struggle of "the juggle". They helped give me both peace and inner strength.

"Make peace with yourself and you make peace with the world." – Charmaine Smith Ladd, 'Shake Hands with Yourself: A Peacemaker's Guide to Happiness & Inner Peace.'

You have got to get rid of the poisonous people in your life in order to keep your core clean. They go hand in hand. You wash your dishes so you don't have to eat on a dirty plate, right? Well, after putting in so much work to clean your core and restore it to a pure condition, why let any poisonous factors in your life do the exact same damage all over again?

It may be hard to change in the beginning, but move those toxic things out of your world. You'll never move forward on your journey if you don't do the work - it just will not happen. (Remember what I said about like attracting like?)

Poisonous people are the very people that turned on you when you were lost. I remember when I separated from people like this, for some reason I always went back and tried to pull them back in. WHY? Maybe it was fear of the unknown and I was scared of taking a leap of faith into a world on my own. Those people were my 'comfort blanket' for a while and although they didn't enhance my life, I knew what to expect from them. Think about the dog that still goes to its owner even though it expects a kicking. The dog knows what to expect, (even though it's not going to be good,) and in some ways that can be easier to deal with than *not* knowing.

Just remember that those people have been removed from your life for a reason. They are spiritually dangerous; they will bring you down. Instead of motivating you and uplifting you, they make you feel sad, uncomfortable, unlovable, and miserable. They will always point out the worst in you. There should be no one in your life that makes you feel low, *especially* when you're trying to rebuild from within. Get them out of your life, and keep them out. If they're not uplifting you, then you need to downgrade them.

You don't need to look for acceptance from the people around you. Remember that you are already accepted by God, who is the creator of all things good. You are accepted by the Creator of the universe, and the One who loves you the most. So why should you worry about being accepted by someone who doesn't have the ability or know-how to wake you from your sleep, give you peace, order your steps or see your dreams through? When I remembered that, I stopped worrying. I *knew* to whom I belonged and it was enough for me.

You're going to face some difficult things as you embark on your path of healing. Don't be afraid to crack yourself open and really evaluate yourself. I know that you may be going through it right now, but there is no problem that God cannot fix. You've got to look within and through faith and prayer you *will* eventually find the strength to face all your problems, insecurities, and pain.

"Pain is a pesky part of being human. I've learned it feels like a stab wound to the heart, something I wish we could all do without, in our lives here. Pain is a sudden hurt that can't be escaped. But then I have also learned that because of pain, I can feel the beauty, tenderness, and freedom of healing. Pain feels like a fast stab wound to the heart. But then healing feels like the wind against your face when you are spreading your wings and flying

through the air! We may not have wings growing out of
our backs, but healing is the closest thing that will give us
that wind against our faces." – C. Joy Bell C.

It took for me to experience the lowest points in my life in 2007, to motivate me to fight back and to begin the better days of my life in subsequent years. J K Rowling famously said, *"Rock bottom became the solid foundation on which I built my life."* And I'm sure that for her it didn't come easily; neither did it for me. I was raising my children, working, and fighting for my life all at the same time. I'm a living witness that it is doable, but I discovered that trying to do it alone was self-defeating. I had to enlist the power of God to lead me and guide me to my better self. And of paramount importance to my living a better life and learning to love myself, was learning self-acceptance.

"Friendship with oneself is all important, because without
it one cannot be friends with anyone else in the world." –
Eleanor Roosevelt.

All our lives, we have this picture in our heads of the person we should be - how we should act, look and feel about certain situations in life. The images can come from anywhere - characters on your favorite TV show, popular girls in school, even hints and suggestions from guys you date. No matter what, it seems like we always look outside of ourselves to define *who and what* we should be.

Clearly that is a mistake, because outside stimuli varies, people's opinions change, and what's hot and in style today is out of style tomorrow. That means who you *think* you should be will constantly change, depending upon what image you're hooked on at the time. That's enough to drive anybody crazy.

And all this outside influence from the media can also be responsible for another whole set of problems which women often face. We're all being bombarded with images of the 'perfect' figure, hair, make-up, lifestyle, boyfriend, children...I could go on and on! And if we feel that we don't somehow measure up to this 'perfect' idea, then we are likely to beat ourselves up over it. And that doesn't mean just feeling bad about ourselves, but can also often mean that we 'punish' ourselves for being less than perfect. This punishment can take many frightening forms such as depression, self-harm, eating disorders and allowing ourselves to be treated badly by others because we are not 'perfect'; we think that's all we deserve or are worthy of. Do you now realize how damaging these outside images can be?

Even while you're learning to accept yourself, you might still compare yourself to others and wonder, "Why has God blessed them with that great thing, and not me?" Realize this: one has absolutely nothing to do with the other, but people who don't accept their *own* lives will often 'peep' into the lives of others for justification. It took me a while but I eventually realized little by little that the *very people* who had something to say about my situation were usually in a situation *far* worse than mine! Just because you can't see what their situation is doesn't mean that it's non-existent. That knowledge gave me the insight and compassion to forgive those folks who had negative things to say about me. I realized that the more a person hurts you, the more they are likely to be hurting on the inside about their own situations. *"Often those that criticise others reveal what he himself lacks."* – Shannon L. Alder

In order to move forward, you have to stop comparing your life to others'. Remember that your story is different to theirs and not everyone progresses at the same speed. Continue to work on loving yourself, and you'll shift from being jealous of other's success to being happy about it. Jealousy comes when you're not truly happy within yourself. People fail to see the story and focus on the glory.

When self is "whole", it's easy to love, genuinely appreciate, and be happy for others climbing their own ladder to success. When you take a step back like this you can appreciate the fact that everyone's journey is different. Some go full steam ahead on the highway to get to where they want to be, while others choose the more scenic route and stop off to admire the view along the way. It is a personal journey for everyone, including myself. I remember wanting to do everything that everyone else was doing, and *that* was my downfall. I never took the time to enjoy the things I was doing. Instead, everything "they" were doing seemed to be more fun.

Truth is, if you want "fun", then you have to *create* fun around yourself. You have to create the life you want to live; you're ultimately responsible for you and no-one else can make things happen for you. It's bad business when you want to live the life of another. Having a mentor or aspiring to be something is one thing, but when you want what others have and wish them harm, then you're dealing with feelings of hatred and jealousy, which are poisonous to your health. Examine why or how the people around you are succeeding, recheck yourself, and make the necessary changes in your life which will lead to loving yourself again instead of being jealous of what others have. It's simply not worth it and will not make you happy in the long term. *"Our envy always lasts longer than the happiness of those we envy."* – François de La Rochefoucauld

It starts with being happy with your own triumphs and successes. Being happy with yourself is key. Life is what you make it. If you don't like it...CHANGE IT! The energy that is used towards being jealous of what others have would be better used to improve upon what you have, and once again, accepting yourself *instead* of putting yourself down.

I was a woman having children out of wedlock, so I can understand your pain. I've been there and I *know* what you're going through. Society did not accept me, so I thought, 'Why should I accept myself?' The fact that none of my children's fathers fought for a deeper relationship with me, or tried to keep me even *after* we conceived children together, furthered my belief that I didn't amount to much. Their rejection gave me more fuel to reject *myself*. If *they* didn't want me then that must have meant that I wasn't worth having, right? WRONG! But I couldn't see that at the time.

The criticism from my parents definitely didn't help either, especially when they came out with, "You haven't seen this in our lifestyle. You'll be on welfare for the rest of your life." My dad even told me to get married to "save face". All of this negativity just reinforced my inner feelings of low self-worth. The *more* you hear that kind of thing, the *more* you believe it. If it wasn't true to begin with, it can become a self-fulfilling prophecy. Think of all those kids who are told they will never amount to nothing; if no-one boosts their self-esteem and explains that there *are* other ways of living life, then the chances are that they *will* amount to nothing. It's a tough hole to climb out of once you believe it's true.

No one *wants* to hear feedback like that. It doesn't help you in the fight to love yourself or to accept who you are. However, this is the turnaround season of your life. When you start seeking the love of God, you can't help but learn how to love and accept you. It's not a grand epiphany, but little by little you should know that God created you. He didn't make any mistakes; He knew *exactly* what He was doing. You're a one-of-a-kind miracle; it shouldn't be hard to accept that. Is there anyone in your circle of friends, on TV, or in society that knows who you are better than God, or how you are *meant* to be? Clearly, the answer is nobody. He knows you inside and out and loves what He sees; after all, He created you so why would He not love you with all of his heart?

Part of learning to accept yourself means that you have to look carefully at your own life and begin to discover what God has put you on earth to do; what is *your* purpose? Why did God create such a special person as you? You're unique and there will never be another one quite like you, so the reason you are here must also be pretty special. I began to embrace myself wholeheartedly because I knew God embraced me with the same enthusiasm.

When you really begin to search your inner self in this way, you'll find that you're so busy trying to discover your true gifts, and what God wants you to accomplish by using them, that you have less time to focus on your shortcomings or flaws. *"The greatest tool of self-love is self-awareness. Once you truly know yourself, love is the only option."* – Vironika Tugaleva.

You will also have less time to be preoccupied by those who appear to have more than you. Accept yourself, and forget about those people who reject your new lifestyle. If they reject you then they have no place in your life. Remember, you're heading into the future with vigor, and the past has no place in this new beginning.

Now it's time to feed and nurture yourself. This is the time to fill your life with joy and bypass the pain. This is the time to lean on God, all while accepting yourself. This is when you begin to care about you, and find worth in yourself. This is the beginning of the greatest love you will ever experience. This is the beginning of loving you.

> *"Believing in yourself is one of the greatest things that you could ever do for yourself. But the greatest lies in loving yourself unconditionally."* – Edmond Mbiaka.

"Dear God, I have accepted that I am yours, but I have trouble accepting that I am Great. God please guide me daily in your will. I want to understand and accept me better. I want to know my purpose and make you proud. God I thank you for accepting me even though I'm not perfect. In Jesus name, Amen."

The Book of Self-worth and True Love

Slowly but surely I began to believe in a better me. I found out what love *really* meant and who loved me the most! I knew that I had to love *me* in order to be able to love anyone else. This was the beginning of my new journey.

But that's easier said than done, right? Yes I believed in a better me, but have you ever tried to walk the walk of the straight and narrow and found that you got squeezed out of the way? So is it easier to just walk the wide road and deal with the wrath of life? Is it? No! *That* is the cowardly way out. And you've not gotten to this stage in your life to be taking that route any longer. Did you think this was going to be easy? Did you think this was going to be the sweetest piece of cake you've ever eaten? Well, I'm sorry, sugar, but you're going to soon find out that this will be the hardest walk ever, but it will also be one of the most worthwhile you've ever taken.

This will be the turning point in your life, and now that you've decided to *love you first* there's gonna be guns loaded with trash, ready and aimed at you on an almost daily basis. And when I talk about these guns, I mean they're gonna be loaded with evil, hate, dream killers, party poopers and the like. There will always be people out there who wish to crush you and your hopes and dreams and I'm sure you know the kind I'm talking about. There will have been the school teacher who told you that you were useless and didn't have the ability to move forward, the so-called friend who spoke about you behind your back after you had shared your most secret moments, expecting them to be kept confidential. There's the family member who looked down their nose at you, the boss who asked if you had put weight on...and the list goes on. These people are toxic and have no place in your life anymore. After all, if they treat others so badly, why would you want to be around them from now on? You are worth far more than their derision.

> *"Remember not to give up; the beginning is always the hardest."* Fortune Cookie.

So to quote The Sound of Music, 'let's start from the very beginning; it's a very good place to start'. You were lost and you got over that with acceptance. Now it's time for you to move forward with self-worth and true love. Let's begin with you, and the power you possess from within. You do you know that you're *more* than a conqueror and you're worth *much more* than gold, right? You simply *have* to have this belief within you that you ARE worth it! God made no-one else quite like you and he has plans for you that start with you gaining some inner strength and self-belief.

I remember not thinking much of myself. There was no waiting on the 'right one' and I freely allowed trash into my innermost temple. In other words, I had sex with folks whose rightful place was in the garbage, and *not* with me! And when I say this, please believe that I'm not trying to degrade anyone; I'm just saying they were *not* the right people for me. Maybe in another place or time they would have been, but *not* at that stage in my life. At this time in my life my self-worth was ... Shucks I had *no* self-worth. I was feeling something more like *worthless*. I tried to soothe my feelings of worthlessness by being with people that clearly *weren't* worth my time.

And I don't just mean sexual partners here; no, I allowed other people into my life that had no feelings or empathy for me, but I mistook their interest for me as something else. I thought they found me funny or interesting and it wasn't until much later that I realized these people were simply using me for what they could get. I didn't realize that then, but looking back now I can see that I was attempting to fill the void within me because if these people wanted to spend time with me, that made me worth being with, right?

> *"When you need to be loved, you take love wherever you*
> *can find it. When you are desperate to be loved, feel love,*
> *know love, you seek out what you think love should look*
> *like. When you find love, or what you think love is, you*
> *will lie, kill, and steal to keep it. But learning about real*
> *love comes from within. It cannot be given. It cannot be*
> *taken away. It grows from your ability to re-create within*
> *yourself, the essence of loving experiences you have had in*
> *your life."* – Iyanla Vanzant

Some of us have issues of lack of self-love and self-worth going back to when we were a lot younger. If you struggled with these issues as a teenager, then you should know that just because you pass that magical mark from 19 to 20 where you are no longer technically a "teen", that doesn't mean the issue isn't still lingering somewhere. If anything, that hurt and pain will cement itself into your life permanently if you let it, so you must face these issues head-on and try to heal from the pain (remember what I said about forgiveness?) as early as possible. Otherwise, it will consume you for years.

As high school years rolled on for me, my anxiety and inward awkwardness continued. For about six months, I became a cutter. I cut myself as a relief—a physical pain, instead of a social or inner pain. It took my mind off of what was going on in my head. I used a razor blade and cut the inside of my forearm. My mom found out about my cutting and was upset.

"Why are you doing that? You need to stop that immediately," she said in fright.

However, it was a male teacher that many students confided in and talked to about issues in their lives who convinced me to stop. It was in the 10th grade, and he convinced me through a series of pep talk sessions that I was smart, beautiful, and that I could be anything that I wanted to be. Today, I still have physical scars from cutting. They remind me of that time in my life and how far I have come.

I was one of the lucky ones though – I managed to stop when I did. I *know* that for some of you that *will* not be the case and this may have been the start of a life-long battle with self-harm. I understand that it becomes your 'friend'; your 'go-to' in times of need, but it's not your friend and it's *not* going to help you in the long term. If you haven't been lucky enough to find someone to help you get through this then I encourage you to start talking to someone, now, TODAY! You *can* get through this with the right 'listening ear' whether that is a trusted friend, a counsellor or simply through talking to God. He will always offer you that listening ear and there will be no negative judgements.

People view and handle casual sex differently. Some people are completely indifferent after a hook-up, while others immediately catch feelings for the other person. No matter how you personally view it, *most* people would agree that casual sex starts off fun, but after a while, (be it days or years,) it eventually has a serious effect on your self-worth. You start asking yourself is it just your body that holds interest...what about your mind? Does anyone get close enough to know the real you, or is it always merely the physical? Your body is your temple, and you have to always ask yourself: "Is this person worthy of touching my most sacred spot? Should they be allowed in here?" Your level of self-worth and self-esteem starts with just that - self, and how well you treat yourself. If you want someone to treat you like a queen, then first you have to treat *yourself* like a queen.

Before I learned that I should love myself, I went all out in exploring sex and sexuality. I hosted parties and sold sex products in an effort to make me feel better about my own personal lifestyle. I climbed up the ladder and built a great name for myself in the business. My clientele were professional women and held elite-status in many communities because of who they were married to, or the positions they held. The money I cashed in was enough to erase any self-doubt or insecurities I was carrying around *for the moment.* During this single mother-of-one period, I was getting my "grown woman on", too. I was able to date and go out with a little planning. However, I wasn't really dating. I was participating in private rendezvous with a guy I met when I first moved to Texas. He typified a Texas tall glass of cool water on a hot summer day! In other words, he was fine: caramel-colored, tall, and chiseled. (Every girl's dreamboat, right?!)

Typically he would come over to my house, or I would go over to his. It should have been a red flag that we rarely went out in public on a date, but the rendezvous held satisfying fixes. A couple of hours alone with "The Mysterious One," (a name given him by my closest cousin and confidant, Mya,) and my grown-lady 'needs' were in order. You know that saying, "All that glitters isn't gold"? I think the majority of us need to constantly remind ourselves of that fact, even as we pray for discernment and guidance. It's so easy to just look at what's on the surface, instead of looking deeper into the *really* important aspects of a person, such as their personality, their goals, and how they treat us. You can be so busy drooling over the yummy goodness that you see on the *outside*, that you completely ignore the bad traits that exist *inside*. Those same traits that you know deep inside that you *don't* want, but I *know* you get lonely sometimes, and flings may occur. These things happen in the real world, but it can be a dangerous game to play.

When you embark on a relationship based on sex, you probably *intend* for the relationship to remain casual, (I know I did,) but sometimes the longing for family and a father-figure for your child can skew your thought processes. This means that you could end up seeking a relationship from someone that *isn't* relationship material. And when you're that desperate to have a relationship, you may decide to start letting your kids see him and be around him, even though he may not have formally committed himself to you, and just sees you as a "friend with benefits". And when that "relationship" ends, you may jump into the arms of a new man and repeat the same cycle, (over and over again). That tends to happen when you have not completed your healing and empowerment. You have to remember that you're too precious to endure that unnecessary drama, and so are your kids. The end result is men coming in and out of your life, and you don't want your kids exposed to, (and growing attached to) men who are not going to be a part of yours (and their) future. It just causes confusion for them and may aggravate abandonment issues they already have.

"You don't buy all the clothes in the market. You choose slowly and carefully, asking the prices for each before buying. The same way you choose your friends, by looking into their lives carefully, before taking any as a companion, then dropping those that are not relevant."–
Michael Bassey Johnson

So where does this come from? Are *you* afraid to be alone, to start this journey out of the box? I know that I was! I was *so* afraid to let it all go. Letting go meant I had to let go of *everything* that made me comfortable, that felt *safe* and known to me. The result? I was UNCOMFORTABLE and afraid. No, it wasn't the best situation, but it was the *only* situation I knew. I was afraid of being out my comfort zone. I was afraid to depend on the unknown. Truth is, as we are *all* afraid of the unknown and have to remember that we are *never* alone. God is with us through it all. Do you remember the poem footprints in the sand? It talks about how there were two sets of footprints that soon became one set. When there was only one set, *that* was when God was carrying him. Do you believe that God can carry you through? He can, but only if you lean on Him.

Imagine this: You're walking in the mall with your child and all of a sudden they decide to ask for something you won't buy. You explain that you're taking them to a toy store to pick out their favorite toy, so they will still be having something special. However, the child completely loses it. You pick them up while they're kicking and screaming and try your best to hold onto them. It's pretty hard isn't it? Well the same scenario can apply with us as grown adults. We might ask God to bring us out of a place of self-worthlessness and then have the audacity to start kicking and screaming when he picks us up! We are telling God that he is not BIG enough to carry us through and that we would do better working on it ourselves. But you haven't done 'better' so far, have you? And neither had I. Ha! Oops I'm sorry to laugh, but that was funny. I remember *thinking* that I had it all under control and I'm sure there are times when you think you have it under control too? Well, understand that *both of us* are dead wrong and we *need* something BIGGER to move on our behalf.

This is the time to really go into that core and pour in the love of God. Fill it up to the brim; don't leave it empty! Remember that the devil makes work for idle hands. "... you cannot shake hands with the Devil and not get sulphur on your sleeve." – Nancy A. Collins. You've already stripped your core clean of all the worthless trash and now it's strictly being filled with love. *This* is where the work begins. Take out a journal and start writing daily entries about love. Not just any old entries about love, but about the **things you love about yourself.** Now let me share with you a few things I've had to overcome about myself. I'm not perfect; I'm a WIP (work in progress) myself. I still write in my journal today.

> *"You can accept or reject the way you are treated by other people, but until you heal the wounds of your past, you will continue to bleed. You can bandage the bleeding with food, with alcohol, with drugs, with work, with cigarettes, with sex, but eventually, it will all ooze through and stain your life. You must find the strength to open the wounds,*

stick your hands inside, pull out the core of the pain that is holding you in your past, the memories, and make peace with them." – Iyanla Vanzant, 'Yesterday, I Cried.'

Loving yourself is a tall order, but it *must* be done in order to truly build a solid foundation and live a joyous life. I'll share things I struggle with, and yes you might laugh at some of them, but for me they were *real* problems and things I *hated* about myself. I didn't like my feet, I thought they were too flat; I didn't like my knees, they knocked (whether I get skinny or not they will *still* knock!); I didn't like my nail beds, because I didn't think they were elongated enough, (yes, absolute foolishness!); I didn't like a *lot* about me. However, I *had* to realize that I was created in the image of my God and that He made me perfect. I *finally* realized that I was the only one in the world that looked like me. There was no mistake in *my* creation and there is definitely *not* a mistake in yours. Do you understand that when you were made that he broke the mold on you? You *aren't* like anyone else on this earth. You are beautiful and unique; God says so and that should be good enough for you!

Now I guess you're thinking, "That's a line you're feeding me". No its not. It's true; everyone is different and the mold is changed every time. It broke each time! YOU ARE AN AMAZING BEING! Own it! **You are Fabulous!** Self-worth and true love comes from this place; this place of understanding who you are, and who loves you the most. This is *what* love is all about. It's all about you. When you start to love yourself more genuinely, you then begin to understand your worth. You *will* understand that you *are* worthy of the best and the greatest. You *are* a jewel.

When you start believing that, you will find that it has a knock-on effect on the rest of your life and you will want to start taking care of yourself in other ways too. Earlier I mentioned the importance of physical health going along with your spiritual and emotional health. It truly has an effect on the amount of control you regain in your life. Little changes can have huge and lasting effects. Your emotional and mental well-being is often tied into how you feel about your appearance. Do you feel that you need to lose a little weight or maybe just gain some control over your eating? Do you find that you turn to alcohol when there doesn't seem to be any answer to your problems? At some stage in our lives, we have all done this. It's almost easier again to bury your head in the sand and go with the 'friend' you already know and love, whether that is food or alcohol. Simply ordering a salad instead of a burger or taking a ten-minute walk can have a lasting effect, and it will make you feel more empowered. When you feel the urge for alcohol, try and take your mind off of it by telling yourself that you can have a drink in ten minutes if you still want one.

Distract yourself for those ten minutes by luxuriating in the things which make us, as women, happy. Take a long soak in a hot bubble bath, paint your nails, try a different hairstyle. These tactics will not only take your mind off alcohol, but will also help with the way you feel about yourself and your outward appearance. You're doing this for *you* and *not* to impress anyone else, so who cares if no-one gets to see the fruit of your efforts? You will and God will, and that's all that matters! It all goes back to loving yourself the way God loves you. Showing and proving to yourself that you *are* worth it. There is nothing wrong with putting some extra energy into changing unhealthy habits into healthy ones.

I would love to be able to tell you that I had had enough of feeling bad about myself and doubting myself, and that I woke up one morning feeling like $1,000 bucks. I wish I decided overnight that I was going to be good to myself and that the insecure, self-doubting Tara would disappear. It would have been nice if it *had* happened that way, but that was not my story. Oftentimes, turning around lifelong habits and thought processes take time. When you're in the process of turning it around, you have to have faith that prayer works. No one has the authority over your life but God. So why waste time allowing people with no power to rule your life choices? No one should have control over your joy!

One day I was listening to Steve Harvey on the radio describing how he talked to his daughters about their bodies. He told them that God created the most precious things hidden deep beyond easily accessible touch. He went on to talk about a woman and how her most precious jewel is not easily accessible either. I found his words very powerful. As women we *have* to protect our body because honestly, it's attached to our self-worth and love for ourselves. The more we let worthless people into our innermost space, the more it chips away at our worth and makes us hate ourselves as opposed to loving ourselves. Well, guess what, you already *have* the tools to learn to love again. You *have* the tools to clean your core. Now it's time to lean on faith, forgive those who hurt you and build a foundation for a life designed to be pure happiness.

"Dear God, I need help understanding that I am uniquely and perfectly crafted with love by you. Sometimes life makes me think I'm not loved and it makes me feel really sad. Dear God, please take the sadness away from me and fill my core with your love, In Jesus name Amen."

The Book of Faith and Forgiveness

The process of loving yourself can be a daunting task. In order to truly love yourself you have to learn to forgive and to live by faith. *Forgiveness* is the ability to let it all go; *faith* is believing in what's clearly NOT there, but coming to the realization that ALL your needs *will* be met, in time.

This is the chapter that will test your ability to believe in what's clearly *not* there and to turn away from, and *love*, all that has harmed you. Yes I said love ALL that has harmed you! Although I realize this may seem like a strange concept, keep on reading and I promise I'll explain. I told you the hard work will now begin and I was *not* joking. It's about to get REAL. And when I mention the word 'faith', think of that as also meaning trust; trust that although you cannot see or hear something, that it is *still* there in your life, trying to help *you* to make it better.

First let's talk about this thing called Faith. I *thought* I had faith when I started this journey. I set out to write my first book and was devastated when it flopped. I thought that since God had given me the idea and I had faith in His word that the book would be a no-brainer success! (Insert the biggest laugh ever here!) James 2:14-26 says *'Faith without works is dead,'* but I paid no heed to that.

I *had* all the faith in the world and because of that I decided that I didn't *need* to work. I never even thought to question myself; faith would be enough to make me hugely successful. Life of leisure? Here I come! Really? How naïve was I? Is that *really* how you become successful? Then poof, (wave of a magic wand!) be successful! I *honestly* thought it was magic but I quickly learned that there is much more to being successful than just faith. I had to work, and I had to work hard. Faith was only *part* of the battle.

The crazy thing about faith is the work involved. While you have faith in God about the work you are doing, what happens when things go wrong and something in your little project goes sour? It will make you feel like quitting immediately. You will feel like God's words were untrue and that he has been deceptive in some way. Well, guess what? The devil just got you to play his game! You always have to look at the big picture. The Faith has to continue; it can't come and go when the going gets tough! You can't pick and choose when you will have Faith; you simply have to have it, come what may!

If God takes the time to download a message into your spirit, it is up to you to have faith in that message and do the work you need to do, no matter *how* many times you think of it as a failure. You have to try, try and try again...however many times it takes, it *will* work out in the end. I never heard of any successful people who became successful without first having experienced failure. So you need to understand that it's all part of the journey. Although the journey may be long and arduous at times, trust that the destination will always be worth it. Sure, it may be long and a rocky road, but keep strong the vision of what the end result will be.

The will of God; karma; the Law of Attraction...call it what you will but the end result is the same, as I mentioned before. You *have* to have faith in whatever you are doing. Tell yourself that it *will* happen. Think positively and you will find that what you put out into the universe, you *will* get back. Take a look at this story about leading star, Jim Carrey.

He began as a stand-up comedian at the young age of 15. His father dropped him off at Toronto's Yuk Yuk's club. He wore a simple yellow suit that his mother made for him. When his debut badly bombed, he had doubts whether he would *ever* make it as an entertainer. But he did persevere, managing to gain popularity. As his dream began to come true he dropped out of high school at just 16 to allow him to concentrate on his career.

He was still only 19 when he went to Hollywood. As many others had found out to their cost, he discovered that Tinseltown was a fickle and elusive beast. In 1985 he was broke and depressed, and headed up into the Hollywood hills in his old beaten-up Toyota. While he was there, he sat looking down onto Los Angeles, daydreaming of his future success and what it might look like. Thinking he could make himself feel better, Carrey had the bright idea of writing himself a check for $10 million. He wrote it out for "acting services rendered," and post-dated it 10 years into the future. He carefully folded it and placed it in his wallet.

Ace Ventura: Pet Detective was made in 1994, followed shortly after by The Mask and Dumb and Dumber, earning Carrey a small fortune. Sadly his father passed away the same year, and Jim retrieved the check from his wallet to place in the casket to be buried with his father.

The point of this story is that what Jim envisaged when he wrote that check actually came true. Believe in your dreams and they WILL happen; have faith.

Now we come to the most difficult parts of faith and forgiveness. Let's talk about having faith in forgiveness! While you can have faith, and work it all day, if you can't forgive anyone who has ever harmed you, you may as well take a seat and stay there! You will not prosper and you will not have *truly* cleaned your core. If you fail to forgive then you are basically allowing yourself to stay stuck in the past. You will have no ability to move forward if you persist on hanging onto these negative feelings. For example, would I ever feel regret about meeting the father of my children even though I was treated badly? NO! I have allowed the negative feelings to go and forgiven any misdeeds against me, because at the end of the day, without that meeting, I wouldn't be privileged to be the mother of my children. While I am *not* saying it is always easy to let these feelings go; I am saying that it is possible. Believe in what God has in store for you, and know that better things are set to come to you in the future and you *will* find the strength to forgive.

Forgiveness is essential if we are to grow into the fullness of who God created us to be loving and forgiving. When we refuse to forgive, we basically insist on setting our standards higher than God's. *'Forgiveness is not about weakening you but about strengthening you to live again and love again, performing at your highest capacity unencumbered by yesterday's maladies."* – T.D. Jakes

And here you were about to get upset with me for telling you to let it go and love the person who hurt you. I'm sure there were some teeth sucking, lip smacking and eye rolling happening right in the midst of that sentence. However, it is important to let it go and live. In order to live you must love. In order to love you HAVE to forgive. They follow each other as sure as day follows night-time.

I promise I understand what you are thinking and what you are going through; I *know* your struggles...I've been there, remember? Let me just take you to a place in my life where I *had* to forgive. When I reconnected with my husband, we were in a whirlwind situation. We made first contact in March and married in May. We did not plan it that way, it just happened, lol! I'll tell you more later on, but right now I want you to understand *who* I had to forgive and *why* I had to forgive them.

My girlfriends knew that I had reconnected with this guy from childhood, but they didn't know how serious it could be. Reg and I decided to get married and so I called all my girlfriends over to tell them what I thought was great news. Truth is I was as nervous as a turkey at Thanksgiving! Remember this was all uncharted territory. I had stripped myself bare of anything which was comfortable to me. I handed 'control' over to God, asking Him for everything and His help to completely guide me through this process. Telling my friends that I was getting married in a week as opposed to 6 months in the future was a doozy!

I know you're probably thinking, *'why should your friends matter and what business is it of theirs that you decide to live your life the way you choose?'* Well, when God puts good people into your life that truly enhance your time on this earth, their opinions *do* matter! (Well, sometimes, lol!) Honestly, when you clean your core and replace trash with good people that enhance your life with the love of God, you know and understand that their opinions come from a place of pure love. They do *not* have any underlying purpose for telling you; there is no hidden agenda. Their fear *for* you and their advice *to* you comes from the heart and because they genuinely care for your future.

So I told them that I was getting married and my friend Eden fell back in her chair, rose again and said "You just hit us with the dude, now you gut punch us with marriage, like that!" (All the while mimicking a boxers upper cut move!) My mouth dropped open and everyone else was in silence. Now at this moment, you may be thinking *'forget her'*, or *'I would be so mad if my friend did that to me'*. And honestly, I *was* a little perturbed, but *not* so much as to not understand that she was coming from a place of love. She was afraid for me because she wanted the best for me. Remember how I told you how people act when they are afraid? And who am I to not understand and forgive her for saying those things? Of course I forgave her and went on to get married. She wasn't going to stop the show *or* make me think twice about my decision.

I had been led by God to do what I was doing and the devil quickly inserted fear into her heart. How do I know it was the devil? Because my other friends' responses were, "Does he tithe? Is he good to the kids; DO you love him?" You see they *understood*. Eden, on the other hand just went with the thoughts revolving around her mind which had been produced by fear. *Of course* I forgave her, and understood the reasons for her reticence.

John 17:1 says, "If your brother or sister sin against you rebuke them, and if they repent, forgive them. Even if they sin against you seven times in a day, and seven times come back saying "I repent" you *must* forgive them."

Did I just hear a lip smack, a mouth open or a "you've got to be kidding?" It's true, I told you: Faith and forgiveness *is* work! When you can forgive the people that do wrong to you, and lean on the faith while doing it, then you are ready to conquer anything! You are *now* ready to build a foundation of pure happiness.

'Dear God, You said that all I needed was the faith of a tiny mustard seed. Well, here I am with that tiny seed. I believe that you can give me everything you promised and I want to be receptive to it. It is, however hard to receive your blessings when I haven't let go of the hurt. Dear God, please help me to forgive those that have hurt me in the past. I want to be forgiving and loving to everyone genuinely. I want to have a clean and pure heart, In Jesus name Amen.'

The Book of Foundation and Prayer

....

"Jeeeeeee-sus!" I'd go into my closet in my bedroom and call on Him as loud and as long as I could. I *knew* there was power in the name of Jesus. I was calling on Him to heal the hurt that I had been through—all of it. I was calling on Him to help me into the new future I so *desperately* wanted and needed.

As you reflect on your transition from the life you are living now, to the one you truly want - the one full of love, happiness, and health, amongst other things - you need to evaluate some factors in your life. Those are the areas where you will need to work on strengthening through positive affirmations and prayer. A few suggestions include: your physical health, spiritual health, and emotional health and they all have their part to play in making you a stronger person so that you can lead your new life the way you deserve to.

In my closet, the children could not hear me, and that was just as well! I didn't want to scare them to death. It was just my way of appealing to the Father that I could not go any further with my life the way it was. It's okay to run out of words to say to the Lord. He already knows your wants and needs anyway. I just needed to call on His supernatural power to heal me and to heal my life and to help me with my life and my children's.

"Jeeeeeee-sus," I'd call out again.

This was my one-word prayer to begin the 'change' phase of my life. It was only one word, but it was *the* most powerful word. I thanked God for the fact that I had a home in which I felt safe and secure. The privacy of my bedroom closet was my refuge. I knew I would not be disturbed in there, and the time I spent alone with God was meditative. I've heard older folks say, *"If you haven't faced anything in life that brings you to your knees, keep living"*. There's a lot of truth in that, *and* the fact that some people have to get to the bottom before they can begin to move back up.

So let's look at things in order. Firstly, your physical health. I have struggled with this all my life. There was a *reason* I was in the closet, calling on Jesus. My physical health was out of control. I had ballooned to 350 pounds and it was taking a huge toll on my life. I tried everything known to man to try and get rid of it but I still struggle. I struggle BIG time. I lost 20, gained 40, lost 60 and gained 75. I just couldn't seem to shake the weight off. I finally decided to have Gastric Bypass surgery. I felt as though it was my last chance and I had to do something that would assist me for the rest of my life. So I made the choice. I was successful enough to lose 80 pounds but plateaued, reverted back to old habits and still battle the weight to this day. I am with you on this. I truly understand the struggle. I will begin again. Will you hop on this journey with me? Can we help each other? Can we encourage one another to make it better physical us? Are you with me? Then lets do it! When you finish the book, hop online at www.taralpaige.com and sign up for the G.L.A.M. weight-loss challenge. We are going to get through this *together*.

When I was alone doing everything, it was hard keeping up with a physical me. It was also very hard keeping up with the mental "Me" too. I struggled with depression and anxiety. Remember I spoke of cutting myself? I also told you that life doesn't change when you go from 19 years old to 20 years old. The only difference is that people EXPECT you to deal with it differently. The truth is, if you don't understand your mental situation, then it becomes more and more difficult to deal with. And to try and explain how you are feeling to anyone else is almost impossible. How can you tell someone when you can't put it into words yourself? That drained feeling you experience, when it's too much of an effort to even brush your teeth, let alone think about preparing a meal. The utter feeling of dread that tomorrow is going to be as bad as today and you don't feel that you can plan for the next week, never mind the next month. I've been there and experienced the bottomless pit that takes a huge effort to climb out of. I remember a time in my life when I would come home, shower and just lay on the couch. I wouldn't move; I couldn't! I was stuck and continually spiraling out of control. I just couldn't seem to muster any bit of energy.

I completely neglected myself mentally and physically. Are you doing the same thing right now? Well neglecting yourself is not going to help your kids in the long run and nor will it make you feel physically able to tackle the road ahead.

Emotional health and spiritual healing are also important. These make up the very core of your being. If you can't connect with others, feel joy or intrinsically motivate yourself, then everything will be neglected. This simply leads to a life of destruction. There are many things you can do to improve your spiritual and emotional health. It's a good idea to seek out groups, friends, and family who are strong in spiritual growth. Although everyone goes through these things and suffer from bad/hard times, *some* have a knack for getting through them better than others.

As I mentioned before, once you throw out the trash and get rid of the negativity around you, *that's* the time to surround yourself with positive people and places to fill the emptiness.

Like attracts like, so if you only have goodness and strength around you, that is what will come into your life, in spades! Seek out someone who is not judgmental, and that you can try to spiritually emulate. Also, read scriptures or positive affirmations that feed your spirit, and help you replenish your strength. For those who may not know where to look or how to start with the Bible, I share with you these two scriptures:

"I have told you these things, so that in me you may have peace. In this world you will have trouble. But take heart, I have overcome the world." – John 16:33

"God is our refuge and strength, and ever present help in trouble." – Psalm 46:1

See the negative energy for what it really is: it's merely a distraction that keeps you from realizing your true purpose. Negativity can divert you from your true path, which may not always be easy, and I understand that you will not always be able to handle every confrontation with grace and patience. Don't beat yourself up. We all have bad days and fall short of the glory of the Lord. You're not the first, and you won't be the last.

The judgment you receive from others can bring on feelings of shame, or make you feel defensive about your situation. That's an understandable reaction. However, here is something you should always remember in those moments when you are about to go off on someone: **No-one** has the power to take you out of your happy place but **you**. If you momentarily lose control and strike back, then you're accepting their judgment of you. This is something you don't need to do, (and shouldn't *allow* yourself to do,) when you've already started making great strides towards a place of self-acceptance, despite what others may think. This is *not* the time to worry about what others may think; that's their problem, their thoughts and they are *not* the same as yours. Just because someone thinks something, doesn't necessarily mean that it's true. In fact, I remember reading a post on Facebook that said "What you think of me is none of my business!"

This is also the time to practice forgiveness on yourself; forgiveness for the mistakes you feel you've made in the past. I had to forgive myself for choosing the men I chose. I know, we all make *many* mistakes involving men. We foolishly take care of them financially sometimes, believing we are "building a future" and "having our man's back" and "being the supportive, ride-or-die chick". Other things you may spend time punishing yourself for include the fact that maybe you didn't finish school; maybe you were disrespectful to your parents or teachers; maybe you stole something as a child; maybe you've told lies you know you shouldn't have done...the list goes on. As I always say, when you hang onto the past, you're unable to move onwards to the future. By all means say sorry, (in your heart and mind if you can't say it out loud,) for your wrongs; accept that you truly wish you hadn't made those mistakes, accept that the past is the past and be ready to move on. This is all part of self-love.

'Love is the greatest gift God has given to us. It's Free!' – Taraji P. Henson

Out of necessity, I believed that my prayers would be answered. Having faith in my prayers meant that I could release a lot of the worry that I had previously kept bottled up inside myself. I realized that when I did worry, I was focusing more on my own ability to fix something, instead of allowing for God's infinite ability to address everything going on in my life.

'In my deepest, darkest moments, what really got me through was a prayer. Sometimes my prayer was 'Help me.' Sometimes a prayer was 'Thank you.' What I've discovered is that intimate connection and communication with my creator will always get me through because I know my support, my help, is just a prayer away.' – Iyanla Vanzant

By finally realizing this and latching firmly onto these ideas, it meant that some of the anxiety in my life began to lessen, and this was a definite plus. After all, it was nearly impossible for me to raise five children and to be jumpy at every loud noise or to tense up every time something unplanned happened; being a parent means expecting the unexpected!

With children, whether they are teens *or* toddlers, there will ALWAYS be something that comes up, which is either unplanned or unscheduled. As a parent, it's essential to be able to roll with the punches. And for me that meant that by believing that my prayers *would* work and *would* be answered, I was able to take things a little more in stride. I reflected back on my own childhood to help me navigate a strong structure and a faith-based lifestyle for my children. Although I had faced many personal challenges while growing up, I strongly trusted my beginnings in the church and my relationship with God as I continued to grow and mature. And I knew that was the kind of life, faith and structure I wanted for *my* children.

My mom would always tell me, "Girl, no matter where you live, you can always find a church." And she was right. From home to Grambling to Atlanta to Arlington, I always found a church home. It was a great way to ground my family's Christian experience, and to find a social outlet that was consistent with my beliefs. And a social outlet is invaluable when you are in a new town or city and don't know anyone. It meant that both myself and my kids had the opportunity to make new friends and meet like-minded Christian people.

In addition to church, my children had Christian schools to help establish and re-inforce their Christian morals and principles. Taylor started in a private Christian school and my little ones attended Christian-based pre-schools. As they grew older, all of the children went to public schools, but they still attend Christian-based summer camps. Whether in a two-parent household or as a single parent, I believe it is wise for all parents to use every sound and principled resource to point their children in the right direction, both morally and spiritually. I don't know a better direction to go in than leaning on God.

Not only was I going boldly to the throne of Jesus, but I continued to teach my children to pray. I think that it is one of the most *valuable* resources that a parent can give a child. Children have their own concerns, too. It can be as simple as wanting a toy for Christmas or questioning why some little girl or boy doesn't like them. They may not sound like much to us with everything we have to worry about, but it's great to let little people know they have a great God to whom they can pray to and express their feelings, safe in the knowledge that there will be no ridicule and no-one laughing at them.

We often prayed in a family circle. My children listened and learned how to pray for each other during this critical family time. Sometimes what they prayed for would be soooo hilarious! For instance, "Dear God please keep my crayons from breaking today", or "Please keep me from talking in class because I always get in trouble", and finally, "Please watch over my foot because Hilton steps on it every day!" How do you tell a child not to pray for their own obstacles? It was funny to me, and I'm sure you found it pretty amusing, but to them, that was the day's dilemma.

It's important that they learn to express the matters of the heart early. I wanted my children to know that they could talk to God about anything and correcting the younger children not to pray about seemingly trivial things like crayons, for example, was *not* tolerated. I didn't touch their conversations with the Almighty and editing their prayers was out of the question. I don't believe there *is* a guide to how to talk to God. I do, however, believe that it's crucially important to talk to him, about anything and everything.

So it's time to just talk. And as I said, this includes everything, the good, the bad *and* the ugly. It doesn't matter what the subject matter is. It has no bearing on God's love for you. Do you think it's a secret to him what you are going through? It's not a secret and you should be open enough to just talk freely to him. This is the beginning of achieving divine intimacy with God. This is the beginning of the greatest relationship you will ever have. Get ready for some real conversations and be prepared also for some solutions.

Now let me get one thing straight, just so's you understand right from the get-go. The solutions might not *always* be what you want, or what you expect. So if you are used to dominating relationships and getting what you want, this is *not* going to be that type of situation. You will always have an opportunity to speak and God will always listen, but be ready for the answer. And just so you know, the saying, *'be careful what you pray for'* is true.

I remember praying for patience, LAWWWWDDDDD HAMMERCY did he show me patience! My thoughts were, 'Lord, I am not made of the same cloth as Job, I'm tapping out of this prayer'. You may be laughing, but I am *so* serious. I quit praying for patience and just started praying for peace. I just wanted to be receptive to his word, tis all. If you think *this* is work, pray for patience and you will think your worst journey is a piece of cake. I tell people all the time that God is THE original King of Comedy. No offense to Steve Harvey, Cedric the Entertainer, D.L. Hughley and the late Bernie Mac. Honestly I'm sure that if you ask either one of these guys they too will agree with me on this one. So now's the time to get ready for something great, a new road, a new relationship and a solid foundation below you, meaning you can move forward with confidence and strength.

'Dear God, I am asking for your guidance in building a solid foundation on your love. I want to understand your love for me so that I can love and pray for others genuinely, In Jesus name Amen.'

CHAPTER SIX

The Book of Intimacy

I n this book I would like to explain to you how I became one with God and the ensuing nature of our relationship. It became an intense and intimate relationship and one which I would wholeheartedly recommend. He is my friend, my guide, and my confidante as well as being my saviour, and his influence had helped me to bring up my children in one of the best ways possible. For sure I had made many mistakes in the past, but once I allowed myself to forgive and move on, my relationship with God changed as I fully understood not only what he wanted from me, but also what he would bring to the life of both myself and my children.

> *"To be a Christian means to forgive the inexcusable*
> *because God has forgiven the inexcusable in you."*–
> C.S. Lewis.

I recognized that I could ask God's forgiveness for my life's mess ups. First of all I was a single mom of 5 and I believed my children were blessings. Yes I had 5 children. I had 4 biological children and one adoptive child. Their conception may not have been planned and was a little unconventional, but *however* they got here was me acting outside of my greatest good besides my adoptive son; it was pure love. Understanding that God forgives when I mess up, meant that I learned to forgive myself, which gave me the strength to look for a better future.

I saw in my future an awesome relationship with God, and I longed for a great relationship with a man. So I desired intimacy both from the physical *and* the supernatural. I wanted a man who would eventually become my husband, and be mine, *all* mine. I longed for that special someone to hold me tight and reassure me that everything was going to be ok. I knew that God had my back, but I wanted someone to cuddle up to me in bed and make me feel safe, secure and loved on earth, as well as by God in Heaven. After I embraced what I wanted in my heart of hearts, I humbly took it to God in prayer.

> *"It is an absolute human certainty that no one can know his own beauty or perceive a sense of his own worth until it has been reflected back to him in the mirror of another loving, caring human being."* – John Joseph Powell, The Secret of Staying in Love.

I encourage you to develop a more intimate relationship with God. Tell Him everything you need to offload. Although

He already knows, He is always happy to listen to you and offer comfort. And in time you will become less and less ashamed about your lifestyle because you will notice that you're becoming more accepting of yourself, your faults and your foibles...we all have them, so there's no shame! Get comfortable with telling God *exactly* what you want in a husband. Keep your prayer specific – although God already *knows* what is in your heart, your detailed prayer reflects that *you* know and are confident about telling Him *exactly* what you want.

A Christian co-worker once told me that it was ok to share with God the intimate desires of my heart. I believed him because of the lifestyle he led. He was always kind, peaceful, and a true gentleman. I later learned that my co-worker was also a pastor. I was sold on his advice. So, I would talk to God about the man I wanted to love me. I left it up to Him to deliver. I had left it up to the Creator of the world; I figured He could work out this matter of the heart for me. I would repeat the prayer that I had started a year before, "I want to meet someone *before* I lose the weight. I want to meet someone who I have known before. I do not want him to be a stranger..." The same prayer I had begun saying in 2007 when my life was at its worst, and from then, this quotation began to mean a lot to me:

"See, don't just look. Your partner is so much more than their appearance. It's how kind their heart is, how lovely they smile, how much they care and have compassion, how generous and giving they are which becomes much more attractive." – Suzan Battah, Five Senses of Romance A Self Help Guide for Gentlemen and Ladies.

As I began to accept myself more and include God in my day to day decisions, my discernment increased. *It's* just as important to know who you can hang with as it is to know who you need to *avoid*. I could almost *feel* when I needed to clear someone else out of my space. I accepted the fact that not everyone had my best interests at heart. For some people, pursuing their own best interest was a license to run over anybody else who may have a different agenda. That's an unacceptable way to chase dreams, and I was no longer interested in being run over by people like that. I learned to pray and seek guidance in order to know the right people to hang around. As my Spirit began to soar, I had to cut loose some dead weight "friends"—the ones with the backhanded compliments; the ones who remembered so well the things I used to do that I no longer participated in; the ones who chose to tell me what I *couldn't* do, as opposed to what I *could* do.

"People tend to be generous when sharing their nonsense, fear, and ignorance. And while they seem quite eager to feed you their negativity, please remember that sometimes the diet we need to be on is a spiritual and emotional one. Be cautious with what you feed your mind and soul. Fuel yourself with positivity and let that fuel propel you into positive action." – Steve Maraboli, Unapologetically You: Reflections on Life and the Human Experience.

Over time, those who needed to be released to their highest good became quite apparent. Limiting or stopping interactions, limiting time for small talk conversations, and cutting off gossip conversations pretty much did the trick. People who I had once spent time with, cultivating their company because I *believed* I needed them in my life were now of no interest or value to me; I had gained clarity regarding the kind of people who would be beneficial to my leading a good life in the eyes of God, (and my children, who were equally important in this equation!)

Men were even easier to keep at the curve. Refusing last minute, late-night dates helped the busters to keep it moving. Sitting at a man's house or my house for initial dates was no longer an option, so broke dudes had to find a new needy chick to impress. Why should I hide away when getting to know a man? They should never be ashamed or unwilling to be seen out with you in public, and nor should they want to visit you at home for the same reason. If they want to get to know the *real* you then they can do it in public. This also means that you are unlikely to get into any kind of awkward sexual situation...those days are gone hunny! Men who could not easily talk about their lives and support their conversation by demonstrating the life they *said* they lived were directed to Hollywood by me - I was no longer interested in the act they were trying to put on.

Whew! I culled my contacts with people to such an extent that I used to pick up my cell phone sometimes just to make sure it was working! I cleared a lot of nonsense off my line and **out of my life**. God works in divine ways and is a God of order. He was ordering my steps to answer my prayers and I knew from then on that when I met a man, it would be one who would cherish and nurture me and want to build a great life with me and the children.

"Your children are not your children. They are sons and daughters of Life's longing for itself. They come through you but not from you. And though they are with you yet they belong not to you.

You may give them your love but not your thoughts,

For they have their own thoughts.

You may house their bodies but not their souls,

For their souls dwell in the house of tomorrow, which you cannot visit, not even in your dreams.

You may strive to be like them, but seek not to make them like you.

For life goes not backward nor tarries with yesterday.

You are the bows from which your children as living arrows are sent forth.

The archer sees the make upon the path of the infinite, and He bends you with His might that His arrows may go swift and far.

Let your bending in the archer's hand be for gladness.

For even as He loves the arrow that flies, He also loves the bow that is stable." – Kahlil Gibran.

While pride may be classed as a sin, I have to say that I have always been proud of my children and their behavior. I've always had compliments from teachers, co-workers, friends at church, and others in our community, about how well-behaved my children are. I always valued my children being God-fearing, respectable, kind and considerate of themselves and others. When others complimented the kids for their good graces, it felt good and was a confirmation that I was on the right track. The energy and effort that it took to teach them good manners and The Golden Rule and about life's many challenges was immeasurable.

> *"What it's like to be a parent: It's one of the hardest things you'll ever do but in exchange it teaches you the meaning of unconditional love."* – Nicholas Sparks, The Wedding.

Be a parent who is committed to helping your child become a caring productive citizen. That means putting your money where your mouth is. Invest time in raising your children and letting them know that you love them. Try your best not to live by the, "do what I say, but not what I do," standard. Exemplify what it means for God to be the head of your life, and what it means for Him to be the head of your household. Make sure you and your children act in alignment with Christian principles in your home: "Love the Lord your God with all your heart and with all your soul and with all your mind. This is the first and greatest commandment. And the second is like it: Love your neighbor as you love yourself" (Matt 22:37-39).

I was determined *that* was what we were going to do in my house, even if it *killed* us sometimes with the differences in ages, and me being the only referee! Some parents might wonder whether it is important to teach our children to pray; I *certainly* think it is. For one thing, it teaches children to have patience, which is something which is often in short supply when they are too young to articulate fully what they want or need. They learn that in prayer, nothing happens immediately; give things time and they *will* come to fruition.

I've learned through prayer that things *will* change as the Bible states, but patience is *necessary* to wait for a while until you receive your answers. Prayer also teachers clarity. There are *so* many ways to interpret answers, but when you pray about something, God will show you the true answers and meanings in a very *concise* way. Teach your kids to pray about *everything*, and to give thanks for the change that's coming.

"There is only one corner of the universe you can be certain of improving, and that's your own self." – Aldous Huxley.

These are the some of the fundamental truths of self-improvement and healing. Knowing that it not only takes time, effort, and patience, but that there will also be setbacks. As long as you recognize that your harmful behaviors are decreasing, and remind yourself that you are getting better by the day, then you'll find yourself experiencing those setbacks less and less. As Christians, we are responsible for knowing the Word and being obedient. I know that God will not bless continued disobedience. With that said, I don't subscribe to strictly Christian music in my home.

I think it is unrealistic to expect any of us to thrive and survive in a world that you only have access to on the outside; you have to experience things at a closer level than that. Just by shutting the door on the outside world does not mean that it no longer exists or that we can ignore the problems going on in it. We deal with the real world, including secular issues, in my home so that we can discuss things openly and develop a Godly response to what's going on in the world. I like to listen carefully to what my children have to say about what's going on in the world as they often have a very different perspective to adults. It's interesting to hear that very few children are aware of the color of a person's skin or their religion or whether they are a part of a so-called 'normal' family; they just don't see the differences that some adults do. It's refreshing to hear them talk about their friends without needing to describe them by color or creed.

"I like to listen. I have learned a great deal from listening carefully. Most people never listen." – Ernest Hemingway.

I learned that as I gripped God tighter, I had to release some of the insecurities, depression, and self-doubt that I had been holding on to for so long. Slowly, I began to trust God more, and release myself from guilt and self-doubt.

"God knows your value; He sees your potential. You may not understand everything you are going through right now. But hold your head up high, knowing that God is in control and he has a great plan and purpose for your life. Your dreams may not have turned out exactly as you'd hoped, but the bible says that God's ways are better and higher than our ways, even when everybody else rejects you, remember, God stands before you with His arms open wide. He always accepts you. He always confirms your value. God sees your two good moves! You are His prized possession. No matter what you go through in life, no matter how many disappointments you suffer, your value in God's eyes always remains the same. You will always be the apple of His eye. He will never give up on you, so don't give up on yourself." – Joel Osteen, Your Best Life Now: 7 Steps to Living at Your Full Potential

If I didn't believe I was worthy of God's support, love and care, how was I going to ask for it for myself and my children? I couldn't "head fake" God. That would just be a total waste of energy, and I was real clear on what a head fake was, and how much of my life I had spent pretending to be one way and I was really another.

'Dear God, I ask that you show me how to be closer to you. I just want to love you and seek your goodness daily. Please be a guiding light so that I can follow your ways and grow closer to you, In Jesus name, Amen.'

The Book of Queen

A s a woman there is a certain standard I should uphold simply because I was born into royalty! I am Great and wonderfully made! We were *all* made in the image of God and perfectly crafted the way he wanted us. We are all Queens! In learning to treat myself as a Queen, I need to know that chivalry is not dead. I must also understand that God didn't craft me so beautifully to be just given to someone who would not have the capacity to treasure my mind, body *and* soul. God loves us so much that he crafted us perfectly. He further shows us his love by crafting the perfect mate to suit *all* of our needs. We just have to remember that through fervent prayer, we will learn how to build a solid foundation and to hold fast to put faith in God to get things right. Our perfect mate is coming!

"A waiting person is a patient person. The word patience means the willingness to stay where we are and live the situation out to the full in the belief that something hidden there will manifest itself to us." – Henri J.M. Nouwen.

I started out in a bad boat; I don't mind admitting to that. I had no concept what it was like to love and be loved in return. I was in another world when it came to men and had little idea as to what a real relationship looked like. If a guy paid attention to me for more than 15 minutes, I thought he was a keeper. Little did I know that men can almost *smell* desperate or insecure women. Shucks, if they were around for that long, (!) I thought it was truly *me* they were interested in. It was *me* alright, but more like a piece of me, (and that wasn't my brain!) So, I had men that were not necessarily good for me, and were selecting me for all the wrong reasons.

When we're young, sometimes we don't exercise the best judgment. I know I didn't look at things back then that I would consider extremely important in my life now. It's all too easy to look at the surface traits of a man, and to forget to actually focus on the important traits that are desirable in a good man. We look at a clean-cut guy and think to ourselves, "Mmm mmm mmm; he is fiiiiiinnnnneeeeeee!" While we're enjoying looking at and admiring the superficial things about a man, we're missing the simple, but true, fact that he is not good for us and that God did not intend for us to be with him.

TV and social media bombard us with all sorts of unrealistic images these days. We see what others perceive to be perfection, and think that we owe it to ourselves to achieve that perfection and to expect it in others. This is a very superficial view of the world and the many different, but equally lovely, types of people there are out there. Don't get hung up on just someone's outward appearance, (although obviously I understand that you need to have some kind of attraction,) but looks fade; a good heart doesn't.

> *"Constantly exposing yourself to popular culture and the mass media will ultimately shape your reality tunnel in ways that are not necessarily conducive to achieving your Soul Purpose and Life Calling. Modern society has generally 'lost the plot'. Slavishly following its false gods and idols makes no sense in a spiritually aware life."* –
> Anthon St. Maarten.

We have to learn to look at men for what they are worth. After all, just the same as women, they are God's work, a masterpiece, a one of kind! However, ask yourself, is this masterpiece missing a piece of the puzzle called me? Am I the one piece which will complete his 'picture'? You have to learn to trust your instincts. You'll *know* instinctively when something is not right, and remember that a woman's intuition never lies.

While things are always exciting at the beginning, you need to look carefully at his behavior *before* you let him get too close. Think of it as almost 'interviewing' someone for a job.

You need to make sure that they have the right credentials, have been trusted by previous employers and didn't leave their last position due to lying or stealing! You get what I mean? Good! The same things apply to your private life as to hiring someone; you need to know you can trust them to do the right thing!

There are signs and red flags that will alert you loud and clear that you need to vacate the premises. Look at how he treats other women in his family, in particular his momma. If a man loves and respects his mother, he is more likely to treat you the same way. *"I know enough to know that no woman should ever marry a man who hated his mother."* Martha Gellhorn, Selected Letters. Other things to look out for include him saying that he can't ever spend time with you, or is always giving excuses about needing to be somewhere else; that's a sign that he's hiding something. If you catch him lying about simple things, such as who he's been calling on his cell, then that's another warning sign. It means he'll lie about bigger things.

Does he have the same spiritual beliefs as you? *"No woman wants to be in submission to a man who isn't in submission to God!"* T.D. Jakes. If he does not uplift you, he's not good enough for you. If he brings you down instead of lifting you up, and is always negative (especially about your dreams and goals), then it's time for him to take a hike! Does he work hard? Is he in a stable position? He should at least have a provider mentality. I'm not saying he has to be rich or anything. However, he should at least have the potential for stability. He should at least be working towards something he aspires to be, not just sitting around doing nothing and making excuses about why he can't get anything done. When you are perfect for the mate, your perfect mate comes to you. Nothing *less* than that will do. And if he can't be that, then he's *not* for you. Period.

It can be scary jumping back out there and trusting your heart with someone. After all, you've been hurt and used before and you don't want to be travelling back down that road! But the chances are that the last time you trusted a man, you hadn't looked for him in the right way; did you meet in a bar? Did you see him while out with your friends and get with him while not really knowing anything about him? Did you 'meet' him on the internet? None of these are really good ways of finding a good man who will treat you right and be your soul-mate. However, when you have the right man that was sent to you by God, you will realize that you have a good man that *will* protect your heart.

Know what your definition of a good man is. Everyone will have a different meaning of what constitutes a 'good' man. I say this because what's good for some may not be good for others. One key thing to remember is this: You will be treated like a Queen *only* when you *demand* to be treated like one. There are many who wouldn't dare step to you and do the work it takes to have you; only the finest need apply for this position! And if they don't treat you like a Queen? You must immediately understand and know that this man is NOT for you!

It doesn't matter which stage of life you're in, your ultimate goal is to step *up* and move *forward*. You can stay stagnant by yourself; no man is needed for that! And there is no need to ask *anyone* to help you walk backwards...that's another thing you can do without any assistance. If it's not a step up, you need to step back!

Here are a few key points to look out for which will help you to know whether you've found a good mate or not:

1. A good mate should treat you well. If you are with a man you should feel protected and secure. And although I know God gives you security, it's good to feel it from your soul-mate too. *"Where does your security lie? Is God your refuge, your hiding place, your stronghold, your shepherd, your counselor, your friend, your redeemer, your saviour, your guide? If He is, you don't need to search any further for security."* – Elisabeth Elliot

2. They should not fight you; you need to work together or you will be pulled apart.

3.   They should not belittle or degrade you; people who do that are insecure in themselves and are striking out to try and make themselves feel better. You don't need that in your life.

4.   They should be uplifting to you and supportive of all your efforts, comforting you even when things go wrong.

5.   It goes without saying that they should be loving/ caring and respectful of you *and* your children.

6.   Chivalry is not dead. They should be polite and exercise manners in how they treat women. There is no reason why, if you are with a man, they should not be opening and closing doors.

     "Chivalry: It's the little boy that kisses my hand, the young man who holds the door open for me, and the old man who tips his hat to me. None of it is a reflection of me, but a reflection of them." – Donna Lynn Hope.

7.   Willing to date you and *not* your body. We all know that a sexual union is an extremely important component of a long and successful relationship. However, ask yourself would he still want to be with you if for some reason you could no longer make love? What if you had a long-term chronic illness? Does he love you for

you and *not* what you can bring to the marital bed?

8. Have the potential to, or be able *already*, to financially support you. I say potential because everyone starts out young and with nothing. We all *have* made and *will* make more mistakes in the future. However, the key is to move past those mistakes and hopefully gain enough knowledge in our journey to help us to step up to higher goals.

9. Ability to communicate: this is crucial. When some men think that they shouldn't show their feelings, and always remain 'strong' and silent, they couldn't be more wrong. We need to know their thoughts and feelings and they should feel able to talk to us about anything. Sure, there will be times when they need the advice of a buddy, but on the whole, try to have no secrets between you and open lines of communication, no matter how difficult the subject matter. Being truthful and communicative is one of the keys to a successful relationship.

10. Willing to give love no matter what; wholeheartedly giving yourself is one of the most important things you can put into a relationship.

You have to know how you *want* to be treated and *demand* that. You've experienced half measures in the past. Now is not the time to have that again. He should treat you like the queen you were born to be. Know your worth and don't be afraid to say no to unworthy acts of your time.

We've all been there! You *know* where. That place where we think we are so in love with this guy and yet he still brings us so much grief. And everyone can see the grief, *except* for you. You can't see it because you have been almost blinded by contentment. However, when you make up your mind that you will live for God, and that you don't *have* to figure out life's challenges all by yourself anymore, then know that *someone* or *something* will show up to test you. That's the way it goes.

As for the man you want in your life? Remember that you are priceless, and should not have to 'settle'. It helps to make a list of traits/characteristics you want in your ideal mate. It's important to *always* have a list of what you want, no matter in which area of life you are talking about. I finally got tired of being number 2 in Mysterious' life, although it took some time to come to that realization. It took some hard praying and some nights of failing the 'temptation' test. I'm talking about the fact that this guy started pulling out the big guns.

I was complaining about us not being seen out in public. And what happened? Not only was I *seen* in public, but we *also* started taking trips. So be ready for the Big Guns to come out when you decide you're ready to step out of your comfort zone. It took me three years to walk away from my comfort zone, but I never lost my faith and I continued to pray for exactly *what* I needed, fully expecting for it to happen. And one day, it did. When I finally realized that I was a Queen for *real*, it was open season for begging.

Oh, did Mysterious beg and beg to come back? Yes he did! In the past, he had called and said all the right words, soothed my soul and made my body tremble. However, *this* was a new day. At that time in my life, I had the strength to sit on the phone, responding with a mere, "Uh huh, yeah... ok," in the softest tone I had. I listened to what now sounded like utter foolishness...nothing short of the comic strip character, Charlie Brown's teacher speaking, "Wah, wah, wah, wah"! Now don't misunderstand me here, I'm not heartless and I *was* feeling *something* about what he was saying, but I was still appalled that he thought it was ok to come at me with this "pillow talk"! He finally finished and, with the biggest smile this side of the equator, I said, "Ok, well gotta go!"

Humph, it sure felt good when I asked God to get rid of something my flesh had previously held on to so tightly! I was over it. Just like that, the three years of prayer and faith finally paid off. I was free and clear from something I never dreamed I would have the strength to shake off. I remember thinking at one point that I could never get rid of him, because I loved him too much! Ha! (There is that laugh again!) Don't underestimate God's power to remove people from your life. That's what turning a situation over to God looks like, and with God I stood. Now that I had rid myself of what *wasn't* needed, I wanted to focus on what I *did* need and want. My desire to have a King in my life.

I remember questioning whether I should pray for certain things when asking for my mate. I thought some things were off limits. Was I wrong! The words say to 'ask and you shall receive'! There are *no* limits on asking. So if you want tall, short, fat, wide, bald, toupee-wearing (you get my drift!), then please know *that* is exactly what you will receive. I'm not saying make your request completely shallow. If your list consists of everything physical, then you aren't ready for a mate anyway. There are characteristics that should stand out much more than physical traits; however there is nothing wrong with having physical desires of your mate. Don't settle for anyone you are not attracted to. That's torture!

I had been involved in the past with men who were not good for me because I was not looking out for myself. I was just pleased somebody wanted to spend some time with me, regardless of their motivations. All of this had to change.

More in touch with the God-spirit within me, I wasn't afraid to admit to myself first that I still yearned for a soul mate. I would imagine in my mind's eye what the man of my dreams would be like. I certainly had enough experience to know what I did *not* want. I had to overcome the guilt that maybe I didn't deserve a husband because I'd had 'husbands' in the Biblical sense, (in that I'd slept with them), but I had *not* married any of them. I had to remember that I was a Queen and nothing less. I asked, I expected, I received and you can do the same.

My problem is I *knew* what was wrong with me. Why were my friends worthy of a husband and yet I wasn't? That's not an issue that concerns me. But be careful what you want from others. I remember watching TD Jakes give an amazing example of this. He had a beautiful black SUV parked outside. He walked around and talked about how clean it was, then he opened the back hatch and it was full of junk. It was completely full from the floors to the ceiling of absolute junk! So be careful about what you *think* you may want. Be specific about you and your needs and desires. In order to do that you have to have a clean core, (empty your SUV trunk!) a solid foundation and be ready for new relationships and a new life.

You can't drive forwards when you're constantly looking in the rear-view mirror:

"I think that the power is the principle. The principle of moving forward, as though you have the confidence to move forward, eventually gives you confidence when you look back and see what you've done."– Robert Downey Jr.

'Dear God, I long to be the crown jewel you've created me to be. Dear God, I know that I am a Queen and now I would like a King created by you to enhance my being. I desire (insert everything you want in a man and DO NOT BE SHY). I pray for patience in waiting on my BOAZ. I know that you will give me exactly what I need. In Jesus name, Amen.'

The Book of Relationship

Now that I had embraced my new title as Queen, I made a decision: if life lasted, there were a few things that I promised myself I would *never* do again.

Lesson 1: Speak up and speak out. I was no longer willing to entertain being physically involved with a man whom I did not feel comfortable with expressing my needs and desires. I was determined *not* to find myself in any type of relationship with a guy whom I had not gotten to know enough to determine his relationship status. And I mean his *real* relationship status here, the one his real life situation actually dictates and *not* the one he told women was true.

In other words, the guy who *says* he's single, but he's really separated from his wife is not *really* single—*especially* the one who has no date for when she will file for the divorce because he has no intentions on filing. That's an example of a man who is still *very much* in a relationship. And bear in mind that you will also hear lots of lies from a guy who is still with someone else. When he tells you that he loves you, isn't he also telling her the same thing? You don't want to be involved with a liar. My Mother always said to me that you can lock your things away from a thief, but how can you lock things away from a liar? There's no way of locking your feelings away to keep them safe is there? So why would I invest time with a guy like that? Not me. Not anymore. All of the men who describe their relationship status as "it's complicated" were off my list. I'm a Queen and I only want to be complemented by a King.

Lesson 2: Friends need not date friends. Now, I believe the foundation for any love relationship is friendship; however, I learned the hard way that weaving from friendship lane to lover's lane and back again is plumb hazardous. A genuine friendship can be ruined by introducing intimacy when there are not enough feelings there to sustain the physical relationship. In my case, it nearly wrecked the friendship, too. I dibbled and dabbled with a friend and 9 months later, I was having a set of twins, alone! It would be 5 years before we would be on speaking terms again.

You also have to bear in mind that when you date your friend, you will already probably have other friends in common. So what happens if your intimate relationship doesn't work? Your mutual friends will be almost 'forced' to choose sides and that's not great for any friendship group. And when you were probably comfortable, (before you got intimate,) with visiting the bathroom together, have you thought about how awkward that can become when you start sleeping together? After all, some things need to remain private! When it didn't work for me I was not angry. I forgave, prayed and waited. Once our relationship was restored as co-parents, we never weaved back and forth again. It simply was not worth it. My experience removed the thought of *that* temptation from me.

Lesson 3: Game recognizes game. If I was ever going to date again, I *had* to understand the games that men played. I knew some of the basics, but after dealing with a man who got married in the middle of our dating, clearly I needed to up my skills! Don't just listen to what they *do* say; listen also to what they *don't* say! If things don't add up then trust your gut instinct which is almost always spot-on. Do they try and make you believe that they are in a high-flying, well-paid job and yet drive a beaten-up old car? Do they say they've got a university education and yet they can't string a cohesive sentence or sensible argument together? Men who blind women with their material possessions and their "skills" may be doing so to keep us from seeing what they are actually all about.

I learned that I was no longer interested in making a man a bigger priority in my life than I was in *his*. A friend's father told me that if a guy calls you at ten o'clock or later for a date, chances are he's already talked to his first choice, his primetime, eight o'clock date—the one he *wants* to be seen around town with. It was my choice to decide if I was going to be the 'primetime' or after-hours lady. I was either going to be the leading lady or supporting actress in this film called life. I was choosing the superstar role from now on. No more late-night creeps for me. No more playing second fiddle and being on the side-lines; I'm worth more and you are too!

I have listed things that I no longer want to deal with, so feel free to follow suit, either adding more to make your list complete, or delete some which might not apply. This journey is all about *you*. I'm simply here to tell you to keep fighting, keep getting back up and don't stop, the battle is already won!

Let's talk about some new things and changes that I was ready for; I think that you too might have a keen eye for these.

Taraji P Henson spoke very candidly on the Wendy Williams show about dating. "Guys don't court anymore. They don't court! Take me out to dinner. Say you're going to pick me up, and a certain time. Dating should be an event. You like the guy, so you want to get pretty for him, so you spend all day at the spa. What happened to that? Some just try to drag you into bed or others think they can just take you to

Chipotle, grill pancakes and then jump in the sack. And it's like, hmmmmmm, I'm worth more than pancakes!"

Exactly! I can take *myself* out for pancakes. Tuh! So allow yourself a few of the following things:

1. **Be Courted:** While this may sound a little old-fashioned, this is a period of time in which you enjoy each other's company by engaging in conversation, attending events, and exploring new destinations together. Allow yourself to be picked up at a certain time and escorted on a date. Get excited about making yourself pretty and enjoy sharing your mind with another individual, and learning all about their life too. Pray before you go. Have faith in what God tells you and be willing to listen to his terms. There will be frogs, but there is a King out there somewhere! For now enjoy being courted!

2. **Have an open heart and open mind:** *"It's funny. No matter how hard you try, you can't close your heart forever. And the minute you open it up, you never know what's going to come in. But when it does, you just have to go for it! Because if you don't, there's no point in being here."* – Kirstie Alley. The new guy is *not* like the old one. Stop comparing the two; no two people are exactly the same and this new guy should not be made to 'pay'

for what the old one did to you. The slate is clean and he is bringing something new and different to the table; understand that and give him a chance. And remember that everyone who has been in your life has been there for a reason, even if you couldn't see it at the time. *"There are no coincidences in life. That person that wandered in and out of your life was there for some purpose, even if they caused you harm. Sometimes, it doesn't make sense the short periods of time we get with people, or the outcomes from their choices. However, if you turn it over to God he promises that you will see the big picture in the hereafter. Nothing is too small to be a mistake."* – Shannon L. Alder. I know I personally passed over some great guys because they didn't have that "bad boy" swag that I *thought* I desired. Once I had cleaned my core, I realized that it wasn't the swag I was looking for; I just wanted the ability to feel secure. So be careful when you throw away a man because he does not have the characteristics you thought he was *supposed* to have. You might be throwing away your blessing. And keep in mind that things don't always 'click' immediately. If you're not sure, accept a second date and give him the benefit of the doubt for the time being. After all, if you have a vase containing 7 roses, and one died, would you throw the rest of the flowers away? No, of course you wouldn't; you would keep the rest and see what happened.

3. **Be Fearless:** *"FEARLESS is getting back up and fighting for what you want over and over again....even though every time you've tried before you've lost."* – Taylor Swift. Jump in feet first and let God do the rest. Why would you be so apprehensive when you have God right beside you and he already knows the outcome of this meeting? All you have to do is continue to be a faithful servant and listen while He orders your steps. I *know* that is easier said than done. Believe me, I have told God to "back off" several times before I just jumped and trusted. Not that I doubted God...well, I *did* doubt God. (I know, but if I didn't give it over to him, I doubted him...PERIOD!) So I've been right where you are! I made it *because* I went for it. It's your turn, so go on, just JUMP!

4. **Listen *and* hear:** There is a difference between listening and actually *hearing*. When I use the word 'listen', I am asking you to really **hear AND take heed** of what is being said. Listen to God's words. Listen to his direction. You know those people that you should have released from your core that have somehow at this point in your journey eased their way back into your life? DO NOT listen to them. At this point you have a choice. You can let them stay in your life if

you want them to, but you **cannot** listen, because if you *do* listen to everything they've said before, you're preparing to allow them, *once again*, to ruin your opportunities for blessings. God does *not* bless mess; you already know this. You have the best guide to greatness, so just listen to the directions and enjoy being great! *"Listen to God with a broken heart. He is not only the doctor who mends it, but also the father who wipes away the tears."* – Criss Jami.

5. **Be a Supporter:** There is nothing worse in the world than getting to know a mate that is full of negative vibes and unsupportive. So he likes to skateboard in his free time but you are afraid to death of this, so instead of you being a cheerleader, you just decide not to be a part of his activity at all. What? Really? Adult, loving relationships are about give and take. The same support and uplift you pray for you to receive is the same that you have to give. This is not about just you anymore; it's about the two of you. Learn to be excited about new things and whether you are scared or not, try them. The memories you will make when trying new things together for the first time are priceless and will remain with you for a long, long time. A supportive atmosphere between the two of you can make you feel like you have finally 'come home'. *"What is home? My favorite definition is "a safe*

place," a place where one is free from attack, a place where one experiences secure relationships and affirmation. It's a place where people share and understand each other. Its relationships are nurturing. The people in it do not need to be perfect; instead, they need to be honest, loving, supportive, recognizing a common humanity that makes all of us vulnerable." – Gladys Hunt, Honey for a Child's Heart: The Imaginative Use of Books in Family Life.

6. **Playing games:** Its time out for games. Be open in how you feel and what you want. The time has long gone where you want to play games with anyone; this time you want a real relationship. The goal in mastering any relationship is to feel as if you can one day be totally vulnerable, (literally *and* figuratively laying yourself bare,) with this person. I'm not saying tell your life story on day one. I'm saying take your time, get to know and understand this person and enjoy *them* understanding *you*. Pray about it non-stop, and if it is wrong, God will tell you. I bet you can think back right now on all the guys that *weren't* right and pin-point the exact moment when you thought, "He's not the right one!" I know I can tell you. I can tell you each one, and why is that? We *know*; God tells us, but we *refuse to listen*. Well there's no time for that anymore. No more games. No games with God and no games with the mate. It's time to receive what you've

prayed for. I already told you to be careful what you pray for. IF a relationship is *not* what you want, then stop praying for it. You will get it eventually and it *will* be work and God will let you know that he was the matchmaker. *"When you don't have honesty in love then there is no communication. Honesty is improvisation of the heart; anything less is a well thought out and rehearsed script."* – Shannon L. Alder.

7. **Let's get physical:** Yes I'm talking about sex. You are welcome to have *all* the sex you want, AFTER he confesses his love for you in front of God and witnesses in a ceremony called marriage. I know it's hard, especially if you have been used to getting physical with guys. As I've said before, I know how it feels to be swept along with the moment. You hear the magic words, (I've got a condom", not, "I love you"!) and BOOM! You're away on the flight of fantasy that this is forever. ('*He must love me if he wants to do this with me, right?*') And I understand how that might feel, because I'm *not* speaking to you from a place where I was a virgin when I got married. I was a having a good time. But that good time broke my spirit, crippled my soul and physically sickened me. It's not just sharing your body. When you give yourself up to a person, the memory of being with them stays with you for life. It's like a dog marking his territory. Don't let anyone

'mark' you. You're *more* than a notch on a belt. You are worthy of the fairytale.

God designed sex for oneness in marriage. ..."*He designed it as a means of intimate communication between a man and a woman who have committed themselves to each other for life. In any other context, the purpose of sex gets twisted". (Sexual Intimacy in Marriage"* – William Cutrer, MD and Sandra Glahn.

Fairytales do exist you know - I dreamed as a little girl that I would have this magical wedding and life would be great. Well, I had a magical wedding, great husband and a good life. In the beginning I knew that God had sent me my husband but NO ONE SAID ANYTHING ABOUT THE DAY AFTER THE WEDDING. *Whaaaaat? You want me to do what? Serve? Follow? Understand? Teach? Pray? Love? Share? Be Submissive? Huh? Hmmmmmm,* (clearing my throat,) *ok God! You got it!*

> "*[To have Faith in Christ] means, of course, trying to do all that He says. There would be no sense in saying you trusted a person if you would not take his advice. Thus if you have really handed yourself over to Him, it must follow that you are trying to obey Him. But trying in a new way, a less worried way. Not doing these things in order to be saved, but because He has begun to save you already. Not hoping to get to Heaven as a reward for your*

actions, but inevitably wanting to act in a certain way because a first faint gleam of Heaven is already inside you." – C.S. Lewis, Mere Christianity.

These are *real* directions that God expects you to follow. At first, I was not hearing it. I *knew* of it, but that didn't mean that I wanted to follow it. I even had great examples of it from my parents and both sets of grandparents, but for me to actually *do* it was a different story. It took prayer. It still takes prayer to this day. You *do not* learn this one day and then discover the next day that it's easy to *actually* do. When you let God in and follow his lead in a relationship, it *is* going to be hard. The enemy is going to start loading that gun again and start shooting all kinds of stuff, (like I mentioned before,) your way. So yes, the fairytale exists. It *is* possible, but you *must* be willing to do the work. God is good and only wants the best for you. Only you can turn your fairytales into a nightmare by continuing to do what you want. Dream and expect it to come true.

'Dear God, I ask that you bless my relationships. Lord, I have a history of inviting people into my life who are unworthy of my company. Help me with discernment. Lord make it plain to me. I only want the best for me. In Jesus name, Amen'.

CHAPTER NINE

The Book of Balance

As we build our new lives ready to move forward into the future, we must continue to seek God. As we continue to seek Him he will continue to give us work. But we must balance it all; we *have* to. The life we have is a blessing. There are lots of things to be seen to every single day; to be involved with your children, continue working in order to put food on the table; finding time for social organizations and church, etc. This is a juggle and sometimes it might be a struggle to keep all the balls in the air, I understand that. We have to balance it all so much that it begins to feel like second nature. Sure, you will have moments of thinking, "I'm too tired to move!" However there could also be moments of thinking, "Lord, I *wish* I had something to do, like work, have kids, have a husband, have friends, etc.!" I understand that there are times in everyone's life when we wish for something we don't already have, but this is about loving what you *do* have, and *not* about wishing for what you *don't* have! This is about being content with who you already are, and finding ways to be ready to receive even more and then balancing it all with the love of God! *"To whom much is given, much is required!"* Be *glad* you're tired! God will open up a window for you and pour you out a blessing which you won't have room for; *find* the room! Be excited about being busy!

The positive changes you make will ultimately affect your outlook on life. How you view everyday tasks will transform, and you'll no longer feel like they are duties– you'll feel *excited* about them. Remember: even though you're making lifestyle changes for the better, the chores haven't changed! If anything, the list may have gotten longer.

It's not about how *many* duties you have to perform as a single parent – it's about the *attitude* you have as you take on those tasks. Choose to see them as *adventures* you're going on with your children. The times where you felt stressed about all the extra activities will be in the past, and you'll start to have fun with your routine, even making a game out of it with your kids.

When I was dealing with my first pregnancy, there was a lady who asked me about the father. She showed me God in the whole situation, explaining that I did not need to bash anyone to handle the situation and she helped me to see that there was no reason to treat the father like a dirt bag or to tell my child anything negative about him.

When I was pregnant with the twins I was very ill and was hospitalized. My friend found out I was admitted, dropped everything (her two toddlers), and ran to sit with me. The next day, another friend came and combed my hair and yet another showed up just to give me the reassurance that I would be ok. My sister/cousin, Khiandra, kept my life together moving my baby shower to the hospital. These sweet people will never know how much they made me smile. There were also church members, neighbors and other family members that came to celebrate what so many thought was useless to celebrate. I felt loved. I felt good. I felt like I had a *place* in this life. The power of loving family and friends is immeasurable.

Time went on and I struggled with the weight of the load that I was trying to balance. I was a working mother and in addition to caring for my own children, I was caring for the children whom I taught. Even with full-time employment and child support coming in, it was not enough to care for my children. We had to use government assistance which was a huge blow to my self-esteem, but life *had* to go on, as will yours too.

You *have* to get out there and *live*. As you expose yourself more to life's experiences and adventures, you'll start to live with purpose, finding things to look forward to and you'll begin to cherish each day. It's about getting to a point where you experience gratitude for the things you *do* have, instead of focusing on what you lack. Gaining this strength will mean that when life *does* throw you a curveball, you *will* have the inner strength and resolve to push through.

Shawn was Taylor's buddy and would play with him. Over time they became a lot closer and Shawn was a regular around our house. Our families had grown together over the years, but nothing could have prepared us for what happened during fall 2009. I received a call from Scharlena, Shawn's sister.

I gave my usual greeting, "Yes ma'am, Suga."

She screamed, "Mama," (she called me mama too). "They saying my momma is dead!"

I screamed back, "What?"

I wanted to know where Shawn he was, and whether he had he been told. She told me that he was at school, and asked if I would meet them there. We met at the school, and Shawn came down the hall happy-go-lucky, without a care in the world. None of us were aware that things would now change forever.

Shawn started staying with us full-time and two weeks later, his grandmother signed over guardianship to me because she just trusted God that it was a good decision to place him in my home. So that's how my family grew from four to five. I knew God would make a way to help me raise Shawn. My parents and friends embraced the idea and no-one said anything negative about my decision. Although it was a struggle to add Shawn to the family structure, God saw us through it.

As a single parent, things may be scary, hectic, and financially tight for you. However, there will be times where God calls on you to lead and help others heal. In those moments, you have to open up your heart completely and accept what God has in store for you. Despite any hardships along the way, what God bestows upon you will always turn out to be a blessing.

There are days where you may feel like you can't carry the entire load, it happens. Having a list of never-ending tasks and no one around to lighten the load can cause the strongest person to throw their hands up and say, "Enough! I can't take it anymore!"

That's why it's vital to surround yourself with a strong support group who will help you to remain positive. Calm, reassuring people in your life will remind you of your strengths and be there when you need them, even if you don't ask for help. That person (or group) will remind you that you're *not* alone, and help reassure you that God is not going to overload you with anything you can't handle.

James 2:14 says, "What good is it, my brothers and sisters, if someone claims to have faith but has no deeds?" So what was the sense in me claiming to have faith in the Lord and what He was doing in my life, if I refused to back up my beliefs with my actions? I was feeling differently and acting differently, leaving the "poor me" attitude behind. I realized that during some of the toughest times, God had sent angels along my path to assist me.

Family can be hugely important but you may be asking, "What if I don't have any family around me?" Remember, there are two types of family: the one you are born with, and the one you create. Family does not always mean blood. Family are the people you can turn to in times of need, who will pick you up when you're down, support you when you feel alone. The people who make you laugh and enjoy life. They can be blood related or not, as long as they have love to give.

I created a family of friends and we all vowed to be there for one another no matter what. Late nights, sick babies, birthday parties, recitals, etc. A family of friends can be more supportive than blood family. I call my network of close friends "my framily", friends who are family. So if you don't have family around you, get excited about creating the "framily" you *want*. Know what traits and characteristics you feel they should or should not have, and surround yourself with people that fit those criteria. Remember, *they* are coming into *your* universe. Just real talk!

Surrounding myself with people like that all helped me to recognize God's blessings in my life—to know when He had showed up by sending His people with a kind word, a helping hand or some other kind of support. I had always loved to entertain and hang out with groups of friends and as I began to feel better about myself, I turned on the hospitality.

I cannot stress *enough* the importance of having a loving network around you, even if it is only two or three people. Just having that warm, supportive energy around you will do wonders on how you live your life. There are many places you can go to find support if you don't have close friends; think support groups, hobby groups and classes. Most churches offer small groups, ministries, classes, and other options. That's a great start a lot of the time.

If you have trouble making friends, reset your friend meter. Think carefully about what makes it hard for you to befriend others. Start simple. Start smiling more. Say hello to others and get involved in groups or organizations around you. Write down a list of things you love to do or would love to try to do, then find groups that explore your wish list.

By the time 2010 rolled around, I had made many strides in my personal life. My children were doing great, and my circle of friends and family was tight and real. I knew exactly who was in my corner and who wasn't. I had fewer problems with who Tara was and what Tara was supposed to do. With my weight loss steadying at about 10 pounds per month for nearly a year, working towards the new physical me was more like a marathon than a sprint. But it's not always the destination that counts; it's also about the journey. Sure, I may have taken a bit of a circuitous journey, but I enjoyed hopping on and off the bus!

Losing weight is hard, let me tell you! Putting it on is far easier! Food is one of life's greatest pleasures. Think back to when you were a child. The chances are that when you were upset or crying, you were given food as a treat to make you 'feel better'. Or when you wanted to celebrate something, there was a cake and rewards of delicious fried chicken, (or whatever your 'thing' is!) Food is immensely pleasurable and rooted in experiences we had as children. How many times have you said, "No-one makes cake like Grandma used to" or "Remember Momma's barbecued ribs"? So what I'm saying is that life is for living and enjoying and if you fall off the wagon when celebrating a special occasion, just make sure you hop right back on straight after!

And maintaining the goodness of life was also a marathon. It was not for the weak at heart and certainly no place for someone who was trying to just get by or fake it. I had to keep marching forward with my family and the Lord in the lead.

Don't be afraid to admit to your children that you made errors in given situations, but reiterate that you want *better* for them. Of course, a child bound and determined to do the wrong thing will suffer the consequences of those poor decisions, and as a parent that reality alone will force you to go boldly to the throne of Jesus to ask for protection for your children, your family, *and* yourself.

My children were good, not just because of the time I put in and the prayer petitions (short ones during the day, moaning and groaning when I felt hopeless, and heart-felt conversations on my knees), but because I also did a lot of punishing and disciplining. That's right. As a solo act, I was judge, jury and punisher with God and my conscience as my guide for my five-pack.

It has been said that if you "spare the rod, you spoil the child". Disciplining your children can be an intimidating part of parenthood. Many single parents carry the guilt of their children not having a father in the home, and feel they have to overcompensate by being extra lenient on them. This is *not* a road you want to go down. As the person ordained by God to raise them and rear them, you *and you alone* have the responsibility of making sure your child becomes a positive, contributing member of society. When they do something wrong, it needs to be corrected immediately, or one day it will be too late. Remember this important saying: *"Watch your actions, they become your habits. Watch your habits, as they become your character. Watch your character, as it becomes your destiny."*

Figuring out how to punish kids to get a desired outcome can be a doozy. No parenting style or discipline method will be the same, mainly because no two kids are the same. Parents with multiple kids may find that what works on one child is completely ineffective on another. It takes trial and error to figure out the best form of discipline that will work for your kids, and patience is key! The answer *isn't* going to come to you overnight, but it *will* come. You simply have to keep at it, and become confident in what works for you.

I'd signed up for this responsibility, so I tapped different resources to help me out. I started reading books, and trying to do what others had done to successfully raise and discipline their children. Sometimes implementing someone else's "tried and true" methods worked in my household, and sometimes it didn't.

My kids are great kids, and I've learned over time that each one is absolutely different and needs different things from me. Thank God, things are working, and discipline remains king. I know that if I don't raise my children and teach them about choices and consequences, the police will. I prefer to keep *that* responsibility in-house.

So yes, it's all about balance; balancing love with discipline; time with your kids, time with God *and* time for yourself; working to pay the bills; keeping your circle strong and true. And I know it's hard, but it's so worthwhile!

"Dear God, I ask that you help me with understanding the new me. I want to love all of me as you do. With a new life come new opportunities and chances to do things differently. God please walk with me through this transition as I balance it all. In Jesus name, Amen."

The Book of New Life

A s you start to see progress in your healing and rebuilding, don't be afraid to toot your own horn. Celebrate! Give yourself some props, pat yourself on the back... sing your praises to the Lord. You deserve it! When you put in hard work towards change, and then actually *see* the differences, taking notice of your improvements will further motivate you to keep going and work even harder. There is nothing wrong or boastful about sharing how proud you are of yourself.

I've had to learn that it's ok to tell the world about your blessings. Sharing your blessings opens the eyes of others, allowing them to see that God can bless them too. Sharing is not bragging or boastful! Show your friends this quotation which should help them to see what you mean: *"Although time seems to fly, it never travels faster than one day at a time. Each day is a new opportunity to live your life to the fullest. In each waking day, you will find scores of blessings and opportunities for positive change. Do not let your TODAY be stolen by the unchangeable past or the indefinite future! Today is a new day!"* – Steve Maraboli, Life, the Truth, and Being Free

As you keep moving forward and seeking further happiness in your life, now is a good time to examine those past moments in your life which brought you true joy and peace. Think carefully about the people who were around you back then, the activities you took part in, and the things you enjoyed. This will help you to shed light on what *truly* brings you joy. Sometimes it is necessary to look back at all the good things which have happened in your life, and bring them forward with you into the present, so that you can carry that joy and peace into your future. That positivity and personal uplifting is what will open you up further to receive more blessings, and prepare you for the mate, the life, and the dreams you have been praying and preparing for. Whatever it is, it's time to enter into your new life and prepare to be blessed. *"The future belongs to those who believe in the beauty of their dreams."* – Eleanor Roosevelt.

Let's step back for a moment and take a quick recap of this book, starting from the beginning. The book of G.L.A.M is all about you. We now know that G.L.A.M stands for 'God Loves All of Me'. You should understand that this means *every bit* of you. Jeremiah 1:5 says *"Before I formed you in the womb I knew you, before you were born I set you apart. I appointed you as a prophet to the nations."* So he loves every morsel of clay he used to craft you.

So you've been lost in the past? So what? I have been too. I *still* find myself stumbling in the lost world. But I learned what to do and now I've given you the tools to come out of that lost space. Now you are able to accept yourself. You have found you, called on Jesus and now realize that you are a perfect being, crafted by a perfect God. You are truly Amazing! You now understand your worth and who you loves you the most. This will give you the strength to move forward and to love others. While loving others, your faith will not be shaken and you will be able to forgive all those that may not love you or those who try to cause you harm. And there's no need for you to worry because God said in Isaiah 54:17: *"No weapon formed against you will prevail and you will refute every tongue that accuses you. This is the heritage of the servants of the Lord and this is their vindication from me. So forgive those that hate you."* Just think of it as haters being God's way of letting you *know* you are doing it right. It's the devil controlling the haters, and *not* God. When you forgive and live, it opens your core up to receive the blessings which come your way through fervent prayer. Your blessings are like building bricks, there to give you a firm foundation for the future.

The great thing about the God we serve is that he blesses us to bless us. He will never take back what he has given to us.

So when you *are* blessed, receive it with thanks and stand firm on it. This is your strong foundation on which your future can be built. More than anything, it is important to be solid in your beliefs, open minded, and to have a clean core in order to obtain that intimate relationship with God. He can't dwell where you keep mess. You shouldn't want him to share that space with mess anyway. He deserves your undivided attention. I know it's hard, and I've mentioned it before. But it is worth the peace, grace, mercy and love that you will receive in return.

When you have a solid relationship with God and accept who you are and prepare yourself to move forward, you have to remember that you were born into royalty. You are a queen. You are a precious and you are worthy of all the things you dream of. All Queens desire a great relationship. You are deserving of the relationship that will complement you, not complete you. You have come full circle and are complete. Believe and know that you *are* worthy of what you are about to receive. Sit back, relax, believe it's coming and enjoy it when it gets here.

Boaz is *not* a figment of your imagination. He was another woman's testimony. God can and *will* send you your Boaz. So who is your modern-day Boaz? What does he look like and what will he bring into your life? What characteristics will he have? God described Boaz as a *'worthy man'* who *'believed in God*,' and so just to reiterate, your Boaz will be something like this:

He should be worthy: He should have a good reputation which has been gained by him proving that he's a man of worth and character and this should be evident by his actions. He should also maintain a solid relationship with God, as this is equally as important to you as a Queen.

He should be a protector: He will protect your purity and respect your boundaries, knowing that sex between the two of you is a sacred act and can only be enjoyed within marriage as God taught us. He will always appreciate your high standards and strive to maintain them. He will guard your heart and make his intentions known when the time is right, never pushing beyond what you are comfortable with. You will always know his true viewpoint and he won't lead you on by just 'hanging out'. He knows he can only enjoy the benefits of your company by accepting the proper responsibility toward you.

He will be a provider: He will work hard to provide all the basic needs that a wife and children might have. And notice, I'm not talking about him keeping you in the lap of luxury; I'm saying that he will have the right priorities and would rather spend money on you and the home, than going for a night out with the guys. He will understand the fact that in a Biblical sense he will be the head of the household and the responsibilities that brings.

He will be observant: He will notice when you have been to the hairdresser/bought a new dress/ shoes, and will compliment you as he knows how important it is to maintain that 'spark' between you. He will know that there is more to you than outward appearances and will cherish the beauty inside, as well as outside, of you. He will understand that a man should want to marry a woman who has the kind of inner loveliness which will not fade with time. He will take the time to find out what makes you tick so that he will understand you fully. He will pay attention to what you enjoy, and that will give him ideas about things he can do just to make you smile.

He will be generous and compassionate with his feelings: He will never look down on others but will instead give them a helping hand up. He will be kind and loving to others as well as you and will always look on people with care, compassion and understanding of the fact that they might be experiencing difficult times.

He will have integrity: He will never lie, cheat or steal from you or anyone else. He will be a man of his word and known for that. He will respect authority and will always listen to advice and kind words from people who are more knowledgeable than he is.

Now I understand that finding a modern-day Boaz may seem like an uphill mountain to climb, but rest safe in the knowledge that the Lord will find him for you, and bring him to you. When you find this man, make sure to say your thanks to God and know that he has found the perfect King to complement you as a Queen. And I want to know about it too; please email me pics and stories and tell me whether or not I am allowed to share. Others need to see and hear your story too. It is valid!

We've come a long way ladies. Oh how we've learned to balance the good with the bad and turn life's struggles into our great juggles. We know that to whom much is given, much is required. I know it might *seem* like you want to give up sometimes, but be steadfast and unmovable! You have a job to do and *only you* can do it. Keep juggling, and one day you will laugh at how easy it is to handle. You will wonder why you ever struggled before. I juggled for four years and still am in awe of myself for getting it all done and being there for all of my children. I know when God is in the plan he will make it all work out good. **You are ready!** You have journeyed through the tough times, and gained the knowledge needed to move forward. Now do it. Walk to the end of the cliff, make the life-changing decision to jump, safe in the knowledge that God is your parachute. (I, for one, will trust *that* parachute any day!) **Enjoy** your new life and thank God daily for bringing you to this new place. It's *your* time to shine. As Rihanna says, "Shine bright like a diamond!" And one last thing before I go, remember that you *are* not, *were* not and *never have* been a diamond in the rough. You were born Great, you were born a diamond!

Now go and Conquer the world G.L.A.M girl!

'Dear God, I am on a journey towards New Life with you by my side. Lord I ask that you always stand by me and guide me through this. Fear is not of you and I will go and conquer the world with your help.

I know G.L.A.M!'

About the Author

Tara L. Paige.

> "What we call our destiny is truly our character and that character can be altered. The knowledge that we are responsible for our actions and attitudes does not need to be discouraging, because it also means that we are free to change this destiny. One is not in bondage to the past, which has shaped our feelings, to race, inheritance, background. All this can be altered if we have the courage to examine how it formed us. We can alter the chemistry provided we have the courage to dissect the elements." –
> Anaïs Nin, The Diary of Anaïs Nin, Vol. 1: 1931-1934.

Today, I am a blessed and happily married mother of eight wonderful children, and an active member of my church and community. I have a fervent passion to teach other women how to become empowered and strong, and longing to 'pass the baton' onto every woman out there who has ever felt downtrodden or not as valuable as her peers. As someone who is now motivated, persistent and excited about life, I can show you how *you too* can become the passionate woman you may have kept buried deep within you, up until NOW! My message is clear and relevant and will leave you excited and invigorated at the prospect of moving forward with your life.

However, it wasn't always like this. It took me a long time to come to the point in my life where I was strong enough to share my message with other women.

As a young woman I may have appeared to others to be a stereotypical young African-American woman with children born out of wedlock. I probably fit the image that you often see in the media: uneducated, promiscuous, government assistance-bound and God-less. I have since learned that many women who are *not* shown a different way will continue in this downward spiral simply because they don't know anything else. Well I am here to show you that there *IS* another way; one which can leave you feeling powerful, strong and moving forward into the future with your head held high.

Although I *was* a single parent on government assistance for a period, I was blessed to earn enough and move off of assistance in due course. Promiscuity didn't make me a single mother of five—insecurity did, along with other issues that I had to work out. I, like many other women in this country, found myself "caught out" with unplanned pregnancies, though to be clear, they were NEVER unwanted babies.

Now, I am college-graduate with both an undergraduate and graduate degree.

Various factors were responsible for my ability to find success in my career, marriage, and family. Self-determination and ethics taught to me as a child drove me, but it was my own steely strength that made me what I am today - a fulfilled woman with a wealth of experience to pass on to you. I will show you what traits women who give back to the world have in common, *and* how to attain them. You **will** be able to trust yourself; **you** will have conviction and *abundance*; you **will** surrender - when the time is right; you **will** receive love and you **will** give back to the world through your actions. I will show you how to do this.

God and I were not strangers. In fact, we were on a first-name basis, and yet I *still* didn't allow His power to help me work through my issues. I floundered, trying to work them out for myself and came up short in a couple of areas that really mattered in my life. I looked in the arms of men for comfort and reassurance, instead of where I *should* have been looking. That led to situations in my life that only my Savior could fix, and when I finally came to *that* realization – it was then that I had the audacity to pray for what I most wanted next—a husband.

Many women believe that a healthy, strapping, God-loving, God-fearing man will simply put a bow on our 'gift box' called life. However, I realized that the answer to my prayer, was just the *beginning* of God showing me what He could do in my life. When society made assumptions about my situation, my lifestyle and my morality, I learned to take those to the Father in prayer. Later when others made assumptions about my happiness and success, (based upon what they saw on the outside,) I learned to take care of *myself* on the inside.

I urge you to read this book if you've ever been told you could not do something. Read this book if you've ever thought that your life choices were beyond God's reach—that surely He would not bless you with anything because you had "messed up" so royally. Read this book if you, like me, have the audacity to ask God to bless you, despite yourself. If you need a pep talk in overcoming obstacles then this book is for **you**. Let my story and my dedication motivate **you**, and point **you** in the right direction. I am a living witness that if He will give me the desires of my heart, He will certainly do it for you. Let's go. After all, what have you got to lose? NOTHING! Yet you have so much to gain.